Finance and Economics Discussion Series: Quantitative Monetary Easing and Risk in Financial Asset Markets

United States Federal Reserve
Board, Takeshi Kimura, David Small

The BiblioGov Project is an effort to expand awareness of the public documents and records of the U.S. Government via print publications. In broadening the public understanding of government and its work, an enlightened democracy can grow and prosper. Ranging from historic Congressional Bills to the most recent Budget of the United States Government, the BiblioGov Project spans a wealth of government information. These works are now made available through an environmentally friendly, print-on-demand basis, using only what is necessary to meet the required demands of an interested public. We invite you to learn of the records of the U.S. Government, heightening the knowledge and debate that can lead from such publications.

Included are the following Collections:

Budget of The United States Government
Presidential Documents
United States Code
Education Reports from ERIC
GAO Reports
History of Bills
House Rules and Manual
Public and Private Laws

Code of Federal Regulations
Congressional Documents
Economic Indicators
Federal Register
Government Manuals
House Journal
Privacy act Issuances
Statutes at Large

Finance and Economics Discussion Series
Divisions of Research & Statistics and Monetary Affairs
Federal Reserve Board, Washington, D.C.

Quantitative Monetary Easing and Risk in
Financial Asset Markets

Takeshi Kimura and David Small

2004-57

Quantitative Monetary Easing and Risk in Financial Asset Markets

Takeshi Kimura[†] and David Small[‡]

September 28, 2004

Abstract

In this paper, we empirically examine the portfolio-rebalancing effects stemming from the policy of "quantitative monetary easing" recently undertaken by the Bank of Japan when the nominal short-term interest rate was virtually at zero. Portfolio-rebalancing effects resulting from the open market purchase of long-term government bonds under this policy have been statistically significant. Our results also show that the portfolio-rebalancing effects were beneficial in that they reduced risk premiums on assets with counter-cyclical returns, such as government and high-grade corporate bonds. But, they may have generated the adverse effects of increasing risk premiums on assets with pro-cyclical returns, such as equities and low-grade corporate bonds. These results are consistent with a CAPM framework in which business-cycle risk importantly affects risk premiums. Our estimates capture only some of the effects of quantitative easing and thus do not imply that the complete set of effects were adverse on net for Japan's economy. However, our analysis counsels caution in accepting the view that, ceteris paribus, a massive large-scale purchase of long-term government bonds by a central bank provides unambiguously positive net benefits to financial markets at zero short-term interest rates.

JEL Classification: E40, E58, G12.

Keywords: Bank of Japan, CAPM, portfolio-rebalancing effect, quantitative
        monetary easing, risk premium, zero interest-rate bound.

We are grateful for helpful discussions and comments from Alan Ahearne, Don Kim, Tatsushi Kurihara, Andrew Levin, Eiji Maeda, Hitoshi Mio, Ichiro Muto, Nobuyuki Oda, Brian Sack, Masaaki Shirakawa, Shigenori Shiratsuka, Eric Swanson, Hiroshi Ugai, and Kenzo Yamamoto, as well as seminar participants at the Federal Reserve Board. We also thank Kinuko Kyousou, Saori Sato and Hitoshi Fuchi for their excellent research assistance. The views expressed herein are those of the authors alone and not necessarily those of the Bank of Japan or the Federal Reserve.

[†] Correspondence: Research and Statistics Department, Bank of Japan, 2-1-1, Nihonbashi-Hongokucho, Chou-ku, Tokyo, 103-8660, Japan. Tel: 81-3-5255-2880, E-mail: takeshi.kimura@boj.or.jp. The author is a senior economist at the Bank of Japan and was a visiting economist in the Division of Monetary Affairs at the Board of Governors of the Federal Reserve System while this paper was written.

[‡] Correspondence: Mail Stop 55, Division of Monetary Affairs, Board of Governors of the Federal Reserve System, 20th and C Streets, NW, Washington, D.C. 20551. Tel: 202-452-2659, E-mail: dsmall@frb.gov.

1. Introduction

In recent years, monetary policymakers have been confronted with the issue of what they can achieve and should do when the short-term nominal interest rate is at, or very near, its lower bound of zero. A host of policy prescriptions have been proposed, focusing on alternative features of financial markets. In particular, monetary policy is commonly thought to have its main effects by affecting expectations of future short-term interest rates. This channel is the basis of many monetary policy prescriptions both away from and at the zero bound.[1] But central bankers and policy analysts have also considered financial-market effects that may be secondary away from the zero bound but may loom larger at the zero bound.[2] One such effect is the "portfolio-rebalancing effect", which stems from the imperfect substitutability of financial assets. A central bank potentially generates such effects by its open market operations.[3] The objective of this paper is to analyze possible portfolio-rebalancing effects stemming from the Bank of Japan's quantitative monetary easing.

When the Bank of Japan initiated quantitative monetary policy easing in March 2001, it expected portfolio-rebalancing effects to help spur the economy. But as stated by Governor Fukui (2003), the expected stimulus to the economy did not seem to materialize:

> ...... one of the effects expected from the introduction of quantitative easing was the so-called "portfolio rebalancing effect." The Bank thought that, even when the marginal value of liquidity services became zero, people would start to rebalance their portfolios by investing in assets with higher marginal values whether these were real or financial assets, if the Bank increased further its provision of liquidity. The aim of this process was thus to generate positive economic momentum, acting, for example, to push up asset prices. So far, however, the effect has not been widely observed. (Fukui, 2003)

One reason why the portfolio-rebalancing effects were seen as ineffective was that the capital positions of the private-sector financial intermediaries had been impaired by an accumulation of nonperforming loans following a fall in asset prices and a

---

[1] See Krugman (2000), Eggertson and Woodford (2003), and Auerbach and Obstfeld (2004).

[2] See, for example, Shirakawa (2002), Bernanke (2000), Clouse et. al. (2003) and Bernanke and Reinhart (2004).

[3] For discussions of portfolio-rebalancing effects, see Tobin (1963, 1969 and 1982); Brunner and Meltzer (1976); Meltzer (1999); and Andres, Lopez-Salido and Nelson (2004).

prolonged recession. As a result, financial institutions may have become more reluctant to take on portfolio risk.[4] Such reluctance was seen as dampening the institutions' demands for risky assets and, thereby, weakening the portfolio-rebalancing effects noted above.

But, we argue that if weakened capital positions made financial institutions more averse to portfolio risk, and in particular to the risk stemming from the business cycle, portfolio-rebalancing effects may have become more, not less, pronounced. The impact of these effects may have been to lower the rates of return on some assets but to raise them for other assets, depending on the asset's behavior over the business cycle.

In our view, portfolio-rebalancing effects that differ across types of assets can be explained by fairly standard risk-diversification motives. As a result of the outright purchase of long-term Japanese Government Bonds (JGBs) by the BOJ, a portion of the holdings of long-term JGBs by investors such as financial institutions is converted to monetary base. Because the return on government bonds (inclusive of capital gains) is negatively correlated with the business cycle, investors perceive their overall exposures to business-cycle risk to have increased. Investors then attempt to increase their holdings of counter-cyclical assets and shrink their holdings of pro-cyclical assets. In this process, the risk premium in interest rates of counter-cyclical assets (such as government bonds and high-grade corporate bonds) decrease, but those of pro-cyclical assets (such as equities and low-grade corporate bonds) increase.

Empirically, we find the magnitude of these adverse portfolio-rebalancing effects on pro-cyclical assets to be small, but statistically significant. When the economy operates safely away from the zero interest rate bound, such adverse side-effects may not be a significant problem because central banks can reduce the risk-free policy rate -- thereby directly reducing one component of interest rates on risky assets and indirectly moderating the business cycle and risk premiums based on business-cycle risk. However, when a central bank faces the zero bound, such side-effects may be more problematic because the central bank's policy rate can not be lowered further.

We also find that quantitative easing affected asset prices by decreasing volatility in some asset markets and helping to lower returns in those markets. Nonetheless, our analysis clearly counsels caution in accepting the view that a massive large-scale

---

[4] See, for example, Muto (2003)

purchase of long-term government bonds by the Bank at the zero bound provides unambiguously positive net benefits to financial markets.

This paper develops as follows. Because the portfolio-rebalancing effects we examine are those stemming from the Bank of Japan's actions and may depend on the economic context of those actions, we first review the design of the Bank's policy of quantitative easing, the policy actions conducted within that framework, and financial market developments over the period of study. In Section 3, based on the Capital Asset Pricing Model (CAPM), we investigate the theoretical foundations of the portfolio-rebalancing effects for which we later provide empirical estimates. Section 4 describes the data and the estimation methodology. Section 5 presents our empirical results, and Section 6 discusses the robustness of our results. Section 7 concludes.

2. Quantitative Easing and Financial Markets Developments

2.1. Quantitative Easing

On March 19, 2001, the Bank of Japan introduced its new quantitative easing procedures for money market operations.[5] At that time, the overnight call rate had almost reached zero and the Bank needed to further combat persistent deflationary pressures.

Quantitative easing consisted of several components. While keeping the overnight call rate close to zero, the Bank targeted the outstanding balance of current accounts held at the Bank.[6] In March 2001, the BOJ raised the target level of the current account balances to around 5 trillion yen, about 1 trillion yen higher than immediately before this change. Subsequently, the BOJ raised the target level in stages to around 30 to 35 trillion yen in January 2004. (See Table 1 and Figure 1.)

In achieving those targets, the Bank also shifted its asset purchases from short-term government debt and towards long-term JGBs -- a shift that would presumably accentuated portfolio-rebalancing effects. In 2003, the Bank purchased a little less than

---

[5] See Fukui (2003) and Shirakawa (2002) for the details of framework of BOJ's quantitative easing.

[6] Current account balances are the analog to reserve balances held at Federal Reserve Banks. But, BOJ's current account balances also include deposits of institutions not subject to the Reserve Requirement System (tanshi companies (money market brokers-cum-dealers), securities companies, etc.)

15 trillion yen worth of long-term JGBs, which was roughly equivalent to half the total value of newly issued government bonds.[7] (See Table 1. See Table 2 for the BOJ's balance sheet.) As a result, by the end of June 2003, the monetary base had increased by about 50 percent since the start of quantitative easing, while the share of the outstanding amount of long-term JGBs in the BOJ's total assets rose from about 40 percent to about 50 percent. As the final component of quantitative easing, the Bank announced that these new procedures would continue until the year-on-year increase in the Consumer Price Index became stably zero or above.

Quantitative easing was expected to have three effects on financial markets. First, it would lower longer-term interest rates because the Bank's announcement that the new policy regime would be maintained until CPI inflation became zero or more would lower expected short-term rates. If this so-called "commitment effect" also contributed to diminishing uncertainty over future short-term interest rates, term premiums also would be reduced and hence longer term rates would be lowered further.[8] Such announcement effects would tend to be reinforced by the observed increase in current account balances.

Second, the abundant provision of liquidity would make money market participants feel more secure about the ongoing availability of funds, thereby preserving financial market stability. Uncertainties about conditions in money markets might, at times, lead to elevated demands for liquidity, boosting the rates of illiquid assets relative to those of liquid assets. In such circumstances, the elevated levels of current account balances would reduce the probability of a liquidity shortage, and consequently would reduce liquidity premiums.[9]

Third, an open market operation by a central bank would change the relative supplies of assets held by the public and, thereby, may lead to changes in the relative prices of assets. This so-called "portfolio-rebalancing effect" has been described as follows:

---

[7] Although the BOJ has not increased its rate of purchase of long-term JGBs since 2003, the stock (outstanding) of long-term JGBs held by the BOJ has continued to increase because the purchase per month is larger than the redemption.

[8] See Okina and Shiratsuka (2003) for the empirical analysis on the commitment effect.

[9] See King (1999, 2002).

Suppose that a representative bank holds multiple assets and rebalances its portfolio so as to maximize its objective function under the constraint of containing overall risk amount below a certain limit. For example, if we assume that a utility function with given absolute risk aversion, the expected return and its variance from the portfolio become explanatory variables of utility. Risk constraint crucially depends on the capital position of the bank. Then, let us think of a case where, as a result of the outright purchase of long-term JGB by the BOJ, a portion of the long-term government holdings of the representative bank is converted to monetary base. The reduction on portfolio risk, that is, interest rate volatility risk of government bonds, generates room for new risk taking, and thus part of monetary base should be converted to some type of risk assets. At equilibrium, utility is kept constant by marginally increasing the amount of holding risk assets, and the marginal increase in the expected profits offsets increased risk. In this rebalancing process, the risk premium of risk asset prices will be decreased. (Oda and Okina, 2001, p. 335)

In relation to the theory of portfolio-rebalancing we develop below, this view consists of two key components. The purchase of JGBs by the BOJ reduces the private sector's overall portfolio risk. In response, investors attempt to rebalance their portfolios in a way that reduces risk premiums across all classes of assets.

2.2. Reaction of Financial Indicators to Quantitative Easing

Amid the unprecedented abundant supply of liquidity, the uncollateralized overnight call rate fell further -- from about 0.25 percent to 0.001 or 0.002 percent, almost literally zero. (See Figure 2 (panel 1).) [10] Even when there were various shocks due to problems in the domestic financial system, terrorist attacks in the United States, and military action in Iraq; a liquidity shortage did not materialize in the money market and short-term interest rates continued to be virtually zero. [11]

The Bank's policy commitment led market participants to believe that short-term interest rates would continue to be zero at least until the actual inflation rate turned positive. As a result, until June 2003, the decline in interest rates spread to even longer-term rates. (See Figure 2 (panel 2).) The yields on five-year JGBs declined from about

---

[10] See Shirakawa (2002) for details. See also Kimura et al. (2003) for the analysis based on macro quarterly data. (Unlike Kimura et al. (2003), our empirical analysis is based on daily data.)

[11] This situation is in marked contrast to that of 1997-98 when the failures of a few large financial institutions triggered concerns about the availability of liquidity at Japanese banks and, as a result, the so-called "Japan premium" expanded and a sharp credit contraction occurred in corporate financing.

5

0.6 percent to the range of 0.1 and 0.2 percent, while those on ten-year JGBs fell from about 1.5 percent to 0.5 percent.

After a period of generally flat economic activity that lasted up until around summer 2003, Japan's economy began to recover gradually, reflecting the steady recovery of the world economy and the associated increase in Japanese exports.

Although quantitative easing supported that improvement of Japan's economy, the Bank's drastic quantitative easing has not been quite strong enough by itself to boost the economy and prices, as stated by Governor Fukui (2003). In particular, it did not seem to have a strong beneficial effect on the corporate financing environment, such as on corporate bond rates. (See Figure 3 (panel 1).) The weakening role of banks as financial intermediaries made it especially important for easier monetary policy to benefit capital markets. However, the spread between interest rates on corporate bonds and risk-free government bonds declined only marginally after March 2001. And those firms that did feel the benefits of monetary easing were limited to those with high credit ratings. Credit spreads on low-grade corporate bonds rose after October 2001.

The prices of other financial assets also did not seem to benefit from quantitative easing. Even after the introduction of quantitative easing, stock prices continued to decline until the summer 2003. (See Figure 3 (panel 2).) As for foreign exchange rates, the yen rate against the dollar depreciated rapidly from November 2001 until February 2002. (See Figure 3 (panel 3).) However, this depreciation seems to be attributable not only to monetary easing but also to a change in the economic outlook; while expectations for recovery of the US economy strengthened, uncertainty over prospects for Japan's economy intensified, including financial system stability. Thereafter, on net, the yen appreciated.

3. Portfolio-Rebalancing Effects and CAPM

If financial asset prices were driven only by expectations of the central bank's policy rate and by the risk of changes in the policy rate, then one might have expected the quantitative easing by the Bank of Japan to have raised all financial asset prices. But as indicated above, some financial asset prices rose while others fell. As we now show, these developments are consistent with portfolio-rebalancing effects.

As shown by Cochrane (2001), many of the commonly used asset pricing models can be derived as special cases of the following pricing equation:

$$p_t = E_t[m_{t+1}x_{t+1}] = \frac{E_t[x_{t+1}]}{r_t^f} + Cov[m_{t+1},x_{t+1}] \; , \qquad (1)$$

$$m_{t+1} = \beta \frac{u'(c_{t+1})}{u'(c_t)} \; , \qquad (2)$$

where x_{t+1} is the amount of payoff in period $t+1$ that can be purchased in period t at the price p_t, and r_t^f is the risk-free gross rate of interest. The parameter β is the subjective discount factor, $u'(c)$ is the marginal utility of consumption, and m_{t+1} is the stochastic discount factor (often called the marginal rate of substitution).[12]

As can be seen in equation 1, asset prices are the sum of two terms. The term $E_t[x_{t+1}]/r_t^f$ is the standard present-value formula in a world with risk neutrality. The other term is an adjustment for risk -- it is the covariance of the payoff of the asset and the stochastic discount factor. As stated by Cochrane:

> ...... the essence of asset pricing is that there are special states of the world in which investors are especially concerned that their portfolios not do badly. They are willing to trade off some overall performance – average return – to make sure that portfolios do not do badly in these particular states of nature. (Cochrane 2001, page 149)

In equations 1 and 2, "bad" states of the world are those in which consumption is low. In such states, the marginal utility of consumption is high and, therefore, m_{t+1} is high. Thus, an asset whose expected payoff $E(x_{t+1})$ is high for expected "bad" states will have a positive value of $Cov[m_{t+1},x_{t+1}]$ -- boosting p_t .

While retaining this general aspect of asset pricing, we employ a model that is more specific in two regards. First, as shown by Cochrane, the CAPM is the special case in which the pricing equation becomes:

$$E[r_t^j - r_t^f] = Cov[r_t^m, r_t^j]\frac{E[r_t^m - r_t^f]}{Var[r_t^m]} \; , \qquad (3)$$

where r_t^j is the return on asset j and r_t^m is the return on the market portfolio. Here, we assume that market portfolio is composed of several kinds of assets, including the

---

[12] See Cochrane (2001), page 15.

monetary base, equities, foreign government bond, low-grade corporate bonds, high-grade corporate bonds and long-term government bonds.

To express this pricing relation in a manner more amenable to our theory and the data we have available, equation 3 can be re-written as:

$$E[r_t^j - r_t^f] = Cov[r_t^m, r_t^j]\frac{E[r_t^m - r_t^f]}{Var[r_t^m]} = \kappa Cov[r_t^m, r_t^j] \,, \qquad (4)$$

where the market price of risk ($E[r_t^m - r_t^f]/Var[r_t^m]$) is set equal to the coefficient of relative risk-aversion (κ), which we assume to be constant.[13] Using the definition of correlation ($\rho[r_t^m, r_t^j]$) to substitute for the covariance yields:

$$E[r_t^j - r_t^f] = \kappa \rho[r_t^m, r_t^j]\sqrt{Var[r_t^j]}\sqrt{Var[r_t^m]} \,. \qquad (5)$$

Equation 5 expresses the excess return for asset j as a function of the standard deviation of its rate of return ($\sqrt{Var[r_t^j]}$) for which we have data and which could potentially capture the effects that quantitative easing has on the volatility of asset markets – as discussed above.

Second, we specify that "bad" states of the world are associated with business cycle downturns. This may be the case in normal circumstances, but may be even more important when a central bank's policy actions are seen as limited because it has driven its policy rate to its lower bound of zero, as recently in Japan. Accordingly, and mainly for expositional ease, we assume ex post returns are governed by:

$$r_t^j = \lambda_0^j + \lambda_1^j Z_t + \varepsilon_t^j \,, \qquad (6)$$

where positive values of Z_t are associated with business cycle upturns and negative values are associated with downturns. Risk that is specific to asset j is captured by ε_t^j. Accordingly, we assume:

$$Cov[Z_t, \varepsilon_t^j] = 0, \forall j \,. \qquad (7)$$

With this specification of asset returns, the return on the market portfolio is:

$$r_t^m = \sum_{j=1}^{N} w_j r_t^j = \lambda_{0,m} + \lambda_{1,m} Z_t + \varepsilon_{m,t} \,, \qquad (8)$$

---

[13] The assumption of constant market price of risk may be derived from the assumption of constant absolute risk aversion (see John Pratt and Kenneth Arrow) and joint normally distributed securities prices. This case has been extensively examined by Lintner (1969, 1970) and is very useful in investigating the relationship among security supplies and prices. See Roley (1979) and Frankel (1985) for its application.

8

where w_j is the share of asset j in the market portfolio, $\lambda_{0,m} = \sum_{j=1}^{N} w_j \lambda_0^j$, $\lambda_{1,m} = \sum_{j=1}^{N} w_j \lambda_1^j$ and $\varepsilon_{m,t} = \sum_{j=1}^{N} w_j \varepsilon_t^j$. Here, we assume that the return on the market portfolio is pro-cyclical, i.e. $\lambda_{1,m} > 0$. Our study of portfolio-rebalancing effects will focus on how changes in the portfolio weights (w_j) can affect asset returns.

Key to our empirical analysis is that classes of assets may differ with regard to the sign of λ_1^j. For example, long-term government bonds (for which we set $j = N$) may have $\lambda_1^N < 0$ because an economic downturn may be associated with falling interest rates and capital gains on such bonds. For equities, an economic downturn may be associated with falling prices and capital losses, implying λ_1^j is greater than λ_1^N and possibly even positive. High-grade bonds may have a value of λ_1^j nearly as negative as the value for government bonds, while low-grade bonds may have a value of λ_1^j similar to that for equities. Indeed, much of the previous literature suggests that high-grade corporate bonds behave like government bonds, but that low-grade corporate bonds are more like equities.[14] For expositional ease, we will assume λ_1^j is strictly negative for both government bonds and high-grade corporate bonds, and is strictly positive for both equities and low-grade corporate bonds.

Effects of Changes in Portfolio Weights on Portfolio Risk

In our model, as in the quote above on page 5, portfolio risk is measured as the variance of the return on the market portfolio -- i.e., the variance of r_t^m -- which is:

$$Var[r_t^m] = \lambda_{1,m}^2 Var[Z_t] + \sum_{j=1}^{N} w_j^2 Var[\varepsilon_t^j] \ . \tag{9}$$

With asset N being long-term government bonds, an open market operation in which the central bank purchases such bonds from the market and creates monetary base as payment can be modeled as a decrease in w_N.[15]

---

[14] See Keim and Stambaugh (1986), Fama and French (1993), and Campbell and Ammer (1993), Kwan (1996), Blume, Keim and Patel (1991).

[15] The change in the share of the monetary base in the market portfolio need not be factored in explicitly because the constraint that $\sum_{j=1}^{N} w_j = 1$ can be used to substitute the monetary-base portfolio share out of the model.

Differentiating $Var[r_t^m]$ with respect to w_N yields:

$$\frac{\partial Var[r_t^m]}{\partial w_N} = 2\lambda_{1,m}\lambda_1^N Var[Z_t] + 2w_N Var[\varepsilon_t^N] \ . \tag{10}$$

The second term on the right is the effect noted in the above quote on page 5. It is positive, implying that a central bank's purchase of long-term government bonds (a decease in w_N) would, ceteris paribus, lower the variance of the market portfolio's return.

But the sign of the first term on the right is the same as the sign of λ_1^N, which we have assumed to be negative. Thus, it may be possible that $\partial Var[r_t^m]/\partial w_N < 0$ so that the initial impact of open market purchases of government bonds (a decrease in w_N) is not to decrease portfolio risk as suggested by the above quote, but to increase portfolio risk. In other words, by taking a countercyclical asset out of the private sector's portfolio, a central bank could increase the overall risk of the private-sector's portfolio.

Effects of Changes in Portfolio Weights on Risk Premiums

Open market operations may also affect how the market diversifies risk by affecting the covariance of returns and, thereby, the correlation ($\rho[r_t^m, r_t^j]$) that appears in equation 5. That the covariance is affected by open market operations is seen by:[16]

$$\frac{\partial Cov[r_t^N, r_t^m]}{\partial w_N} = (\lambda_1^N \lambda_1^N + \lambda_{1,m}) Var[Z_t] + Var[\varepsilon_t^N] > 0 \ , \tag{11}$$

$$\frac{\partial Cov[r_t^j, r_t^m]}{\partial w_N} = \lambda_1^j \lambda_1^N Var[Z_t] \gtreqless 0 \ as \ \lambda_1^j \lesseqgtr 0, \ \forall j \neq N \ . \tag{12}$$

Open market purchases of long-term government bonds (decreases in w_N) will decrease the covariance between the return on the market portfolio and the return on long-term government bonds (by equation 11, assuming $\lambda_{1,m} > 0$). But, as equation 12 shows, such purchases will increase the covariance between the return on the market portfolio and the return on an asset j for which $\lambda_1^j > 0$.

---

[16] See the Appendix for a derivation of equations 11 and 12.

An Alternative View of Quantitative Easing

Based on equations 10 through 12, it is possible to provide a view of quantitative easing that differs significantly from the view noted on page 5 and that is consistent, in general terms, with the evidence presented in Section 2.2 from Japanese financial markets:

> *Suppose that a representative agent holds multiple assets and rebalances its portfolio so as to maximize its objective function as modeled within CAPM. Then let us think of a case where, as a result of the outright purchase of long-term JGBs by the BOJ, a portion of the long-term government holdings of the representative agent is converted to monetary base. Because the return on currently-held government bonds is negatively correlated with the business cycle, the representative agent perceives his exposure to business cycle risk to have increased. The agent will then attempt to increase his holdings of counter-cyclical assets and shrink his holdings of pro-cyclical assets. In this process, the risk premium of counter-cyclical asset prices will be decreased and those of pro-cyclical assets will be increased.*

Reduced-Form Estimation Equations

In specifying a regression equation that tests for the effects of quantitative easing, we linearize equation 5 by means of a Taylor expansion, which yields:

$$E[r_t^j - r_t^f] \cong A_0^j + A_1^j \rho[r_t^m, r_t^j]^\Delta + A_2^j \sqrt{Var[r_t^j]}^\Delta + A_3^j \sqrt{Var[r_t^m]}^\Delta \,, \qquad (13)$$

where the superscript Δ indicates the variable is measured as a deviation from the value around which the Taylor approximation was taken. As shown in the Appendix, the signs of the coefficients are:

- $A_1^j > 0$, implying that an increase in the correlation of an asset's return with that of the market will tend to increase the risk premium on that asset.

- $\text{sign}(A_0^j) = \text{sign}(A_2^j) = \text{sign}(A_3^j) = \text{sign}(\rho[r_t^m, r_t^j])$, implying that the correlation between the return on an asset and the return on the market portfolio determines whether changes in other characteristics of the asset increase or decrease the risk premium of that asset. For example, a higher volatility of an asset's return will raise (lower) the excess return for that asset if that asset's return is positively (negatively) correlated with the return on the market portfolio.

11

In implementing equation 13 as a regression equation, we have data on measures of the dependent variable and $\sqrt{Var[r_t^j]}$.[17] Not having measures of $\rho[r_t^m, r_t^j]$ and $\sqrt{Var[r_t^m]}$, we assume they are affected linearly by quantitative easing. Accordingly, the reduced-form regression equation we use for the risk premiums is:

$$E[r_t^j - r_t^f] = \alpha_j \sqrt{Var[r_t^j]} + \beta_{QE}^j QE_t + c + \xi_t^j,$$ (14)

where $\alpha_j = \lambda_2^j$, $\quad \beta_{QE}^j = -\left(\lambda_1^j \frac{\partial \rho[r_t^m, r_t^j]}{\partial w_N} + \lambda_3^j \frac{\partial \sqrt{Var[r_t^m]}}{\partial w_N} \right)$.

The coefficient β_{QE}^j captures the effect of quantitative easing through its effects on $\rho[r_t^m, r_t^j]$ and $\sqrt{Var[r_t^m]}$. That is, quantitative easing and any associated rebalancing effects may affect excess returns through effects on the degree of the linear relation between r_t^j and r_t^m, i.e. $\rho[r_t^m, r_t^j]$, and on the amount of risk in financial markets ($\sqrt{Var[r_t^m]}$).

An advantage of having $\sqrt{Var[r_t^j]}$ as an independent variable is not only that it is a component of $Cov[r_t^m, r_t^j]$, but also that it captures two effects of quantitative easing that are independent of the portfolio-rebalancing effect and that are noted above on page 4 - - the commitment to use quantitative easing until inflation is at least zero percent and the abundant provision of reserves may reduce the volatility of short rates. Also, $\sqrt{Var[r_t^j]}$ does not depend on the portfolio weight w_j. Accordingly, using it as an independent variable will help provide better estimates of the portfolio-rebalancing effects through the estimate of β_{QE}^j.

As indicated by the view presented on page 11, we would expect increases in quantitative easing (increases in open market purchases of government bonds) to decrease risk premiums on assets whose returns are counter-cyclical ($\lambda_1^j < 0$), implying $\beta_{QE}^j < 0$ for such assets. Conversely, increases in quantitative easing could tend to increase risk premiums on pro-cyclical assets ($\lambda_1^j > 0$), implying $\beta_{QE}^j > 0$ for such assets.[18]

---

[17] The data is discussed in more detail below in Section 4.

[18] See the Appendix for a derivation of the sign of β_{QE}^j.

12

Also, quantitative easing can affect the volatility of rates of return $\sqrt{Var[r_t^j]}$.
Accordingly, we regress:

$$\sqrt{Var[r_t^j]} = \rho_v \sqrt{Var[r_{t-1}^j]} + \beta_v^j QE_t + c_v + \mu_t^j \ . \tag{15}$$

Because the volatility of an asset return depends on both uncertainty about the business
cycle ($Var[Z_t]$) and uncertainty about each financial market condition ($Var[\varepsilon_t^j]$),
quantitative easing will affect the volatility of rates of return $\sqrt{Var[r_t^j]}$ by reducing these
two uncertainties.[19] For example, regarding the business-cycle risk, the Bank of Japan
(2003a) has pointed out that quantitative easing has secured financial market stability by
the ample provision of liquidity and may have contributed to preventing the economy
from falling into a deflationary spiral. This results in the decrease in the uncertainty
about the macroeconomy, and therefore, we would expect $\beta_v^j < 0$.

In equation 15, we also include lagged volatility as an explanatory variable
because volatility measures of financial assets are highly persistent in general. This
model is consistent with the volatility clustering often seen in financial returns data,
where large changes in returns are likely to be followed by further large changes.

Taking into account both equations 14 and 15, the total effect of the quantitative
easing on the risk premium is measured as

$$\beta_{QE}^j + \frac{\beta_v^j}{1 - \rho_v} \alpha_j \ , \tag{16}$$

where the first term denotes the direct effect and the second term denotes the indirect
effect through the change in volatility.

4. Data and Estimation Methodology

4.1. Data

To test whether the effects of open market operations on an asset's return (i.e. the sign
of β_{QE}^j) depends on the correlation of the asset's return with the business cycle, we
estimate the effect of quantitative easing on the prices of three types of financial assets:

---

[19] From equation 6, we have:

$$\sqrt{Var[r_t^j]} = \sqrt{(\lambda_1^j)^2 Var[Z_t] + Var[\varepsilon_t^j]} \ .$$

(1) equities, (2) foreign exchange, and (3) several grades of corporate bonds. Our estimation is based on daily data beginning on January 21, 2000 and ending on March 31, 2004. As seen in Figure 1, from the end of December 1999 through the beginning of January 2000, the BOJ increased current account balances very significantly. However, this increase was in response to the surge in the precautionary demand for money caused by the date change to Y2K and not part of the quantitative easing policy. Accordingly, our sample period starts in January 21, 2000.

Measures of Asset Returns

[1] Stock Returns

We define the expected return from holding stock for k business days as:

$$E_t[r_t^s] = E_t\left[\ln(P_{t+k}) - \ln(P_t)\right].$$

where P_t is the closing price of the Nikkei Stock Average on day t. We measure the monthly stock return r_t^s setting $k = 22$. Thus we construct a daily time series in which each term is a moving average of future daily returns. The Treasury Bill repo rate (repurchase agreement, 1 month) is used as the risk free rate r_t^f. Figure 4 (panel 1) shows the ex-post risk premium $r_t^s - r_t^f$, which is the variable used as the dependent variable in the regression.[20]

[2] Forward Exchange Risk Premium

The risk premium in the foreign exchange rate market, assuming uncovered interest parity, is defined as the difference between the expected returns on investing in foreign and domestic assets.

$$E_t[s_{t+k}] - s_t + i_t^{US} - i_t^{JP} = \text{time-varying risk premium}. \tag{17}$$

Here, s_t is the logarithm of the spot exchange rate and i_t^{US} is the interest rate in the United States. The variable $E_t[s_{t+k}] - s_t + i_t^{US}$ denotes the expected return on investing in the U.S. market, which corresponds to the return on the risky asset, $E[r_t^j]$, in equation

---

[20] The stock return (1 month) is annualized to be compatible with risk free rate (TB repo rate). Since we use daily data in this analysis, we do not adjust the dividends in calculating the stock return. Therefore, as shown in Figure 4 (panel 1), the mean of ex-post risk premium is not necessarily positive. However, excluding dividends does not bias our empirical results, because we can assume that the payments of dividends are uncorrelated with the BOJ's open market operations and that the effects of dividends are adjusted through the constant term in the estimation.

14. The variable i_t^{JP} is the interest rate in Japan, which corresponds to risk-free rate of interest r_t^f. Substituting the covered interest parity condition into equation 17 leads to

$$E_t[s_{t+k}] - f_{t,k} = \text{time-varying risk premium},\qquad\qquad (18)$$

where $f_{t,k}$ is the logarithm of the k-period forward exchange rate. We analyze the forward rate with 1 month maturity ($k = 22$) at Tokyo market.[21] Figure 4 (panel 2) shows the ex-post risk premium $s_{t+k} - f_{t,k}$.

[3] Corporate bond returns

We use the observed credit spread as a measure of the excess return for the corporate bonds. In theory, the two are not equal because a credit spread includes not only the excess return but also the expected default rate. As a result, the inclusion of the expected default rate could lead to biased estimates of the portfolio-rebalancing effects. Since it is very difficult to extract the risk premium on daily basis from credit spreads, we correct for this problem (as in equation 25 below) by including an interest rate in the regression as an explanatory variable for the expected default rate.[22]

Although we focus on the excess return by excluding the effect of the expected default rate, the default rate remains an important determinant of excess returns because it is a stochastic variable and likely correlated with the business cycle. Owing to the uncertainty of the business cycle, investors face the uncertainty about future changes in the expected default rate and hence in the market value of corporate bonds. As a result, investors demand a risk premium that, in part, reflects this default risk. Elton, et al. (2001) finds this risk premium is a large component of credit spreads.[23] More specifically, we would expect that the lower is the grade of corporate bond, the higher is the correlation of the default rate with the business cycle. Therefore, investors demand higher risk premiums to cover business-cycle risk for lower-grade-corporate bonds than they do for higher-grade corporate bonds.

Below, the credit spread, CS_t^i, for corporate bond of type i at date t is defined as the difference between the yield of bond i and the associated yield on the Japan's

---

[21] Forward rates are average central rates between offers and bids collected from several brokers at 3:30 p.m. Spot rates are central rates based on offer and bid rates by inter-bank market participants at 5:00 p.m. (Data source: Bank of Japan)

[22] See footnote 31 below for the relationship between an interest rate and expected default rate.

[23] See Elton (1999) and Elton et al. (2001).

government bond at the same maturity. We analyze the credit spreads for three rating categories by Moodys (Aa, A, and Baa) and three maturities (1 year, 3 years, and 5 years). Figure 4 (panel 3) shows the credit spreads with 5-year maturities.

Measures of Volatilities

In estimating equations 14 and 15, one measure of the volatility of stock prices ($\sqrt{Var[r_t^i]}$) that we use is the implied volatility (IV_t^s) from option prices from the Nikkei Stock Average.[24] Implied volatility of the exchange rate (IV_t^e) is derived from exchange rate option prices.[25] Figure 5 (panel 2) shows these implied volatilities. Unfortunately, however, implied volatilities are not available for corporate bond prices. Thus, we also use the best available substitute: historical volatilities (HV_t^i) and implied volatilities of stock price index (IV_t^s). In general, volatility measures are highly persistent, so historical volatilities have some information on future volatility -- information which investors recognize.[26] Figure 5 (panel 3) shows the historical volatilities of credit spreads. In addition, the implied volatilities of stock prices will explain the risk premium for corporate bond prices if the source of the risk premium for corporate bond prices partly reflects a systematic co-movement with stock prices.[27]

Measures of Quantitative Easing

As alternative measures of quantitative easing, we use the outstanding amount of current account balances (CA_t), the BOJ's main operating target, and the outstanding amount of outright purchases of long-term JGBs (OP_t) by the BOJ.

The advantage of using CA_t rather than OP_t is that we have daily data on CA_t through March 31, 2004, whereas the daily data available for OP_t ends in June 30, 2003. However, OP_t has the advantage that it is more directly applicable to the theory developed above regarding portfolio-rebalancing effects: OP_t includes only long-term

---

[24] Implied volatility (1 month, annualized rate) is an average between call and put prices at 3:30 p.m. each day.

[25] Implied volatilities (1 month, annualized rate) are average options trading central rates between offers and bids collected from market participants at 3:30 p.m. each day. (Data source: Bank of Japan)

[26] Here, we use a historical volatility of the credit spread over the past five business days. To check the robustness, we also used a historical volatility of the credit spreads over the past ten business days. But, the main results do not change.

[27] See Elton (1999) and Elton et al. (2001). Collin-Dufresne et al. (2001) also use implied volatilities of stock prices as a proxy in their analysis on the determinants of credit spreads.

JGBs, while CA_t results from purchasing not only long-term JGBs but also short-term JGBs. But over our sample period, the increase in CA_t is indicative of an increase in OP_t because the BOJ shifted its composition of holdings of JGBs toward longer maturity instruments. Figure 6 (panel 1) displays the BOJ's balance sheet at the end of each month. As seen in the figure, OP_t generally track CA_t balances over this period.

One limitation that applies to both CA_t and OP_t is that they are measured in terms of yen, whereas a measure that would more closely align with the study of portfolio-rebalancing effects would be in terms of portfolio shares. But measures of portfolio shares suffer from the lack of reliable measures of the value of the market portfolio. Available data indicate that movements in relative holdings of long-term JGBs by the BOJ changed in line with OP_t and CA_t. The bold line entitled "BOJ share [1]" in Figure 6 (panel 2) shows the BOJ's holdings of central government securities (JGBs), which include both long-term and short-term bonds, as a percent of those held outside both the general government and other public sector entities (public financial institutions and postal savings). As shown, the BOJ's relative holdings increased over the period of quantitative easing. Data are not available to construct a similar measure of holdings of only long-term JGBs, but such a measure is available if the holdings of the general government and other public sector entities are included. That measure is shown by the thin line entitled "BOJ share [2]" in Figure 6 (panel 2) and it too increases over the period of quantitative easing. Accordingly, this figure gives some indication that changes in the relative holdings of long-term JGBs by the private sector were negatively correlated with OP_t and CA_t.

4.2. Estimation Methodology

Due to differences in the availability of data and in the properties of the prices across the types of assets included in this study, the details of the models to be estimated differ across the financial assets, although the fundamental features explained in section 3 are shared by all the models.

Return and Volatility of Stocks

Replacing the ex ante return $E_t[r_t^s]$ with the ex post return r_t^s in equation 14, we estimate the following model using generalized method of moments (GMM).

17

$$r_t^s - r_t^f = \alpha(IV_t^s) + \beta(CA_t) + \gamma(OP_t) + c + \xi_t^s, \tag{19}$$

where $\xi_t^s \equiv r_t^s - E_t[r_t^s]$ is a forecast error of stock return. Since under rational expectations the error in the forecast of r_t^s is uncorrelated with information dated t and earlier, it follows that

$$E_t[\xi_t^s z_t] = 0, \tag{20}$$

where z_t is a vector of variables dated t and earlier (and, thus, orthogonal to the excess return surprise in period $t+1$ and later). The orthogonality condition given by equation 20 then forms the basis for estimating the model via GMM. Because the forecast error ξ_t follows a moving average process of order $k-1$, $k-1$ autocorrelation terms are used in computing the covariance matrix of the orthogonality conditions. (Recall that we analyze the monthly stock return and set $k = 22$.)

To estimate the effect of quantitative easing on implied volatility, we re-write equation 15 as follows:

$$IV_t^s = \rho_v(IV_{t-1}^s) + \beta_v CA_t + \gamma_v OP_t + c_v + \mu_t^s. \tag{21}$$

The parameters of a system of equations 19 and 21 are estimated using GMM. To avoid multicollinearity, we separately estimate the effects of OP_t and CA_t.[28]

To check the sensitivity of the results to the estimation method, equations 19 and 21 are estimated with an alternative assumption regarding the error term. Specifically, we estimate the following equation using least squares:

$$r_t^s - r_t^f = \alpha(IV_{t-1}^s) + \beta(CA_t) + \gamma(OP_t) + c + \sum_{i=0}^{k}\omega_i \varepsilon_{t+k-i}, \tag{22}$$

where ε_t is a serially uncorrelated white noise process and ω_i are the moving average parameters.[29] We also estimate equation 21 under the assumption that μ_t^s follows a GARCH(1,1) process.

---

[28] In estimating both forward exchange risk premium and credit spreads, we also separate the effect of the increase in the current accounts and the effect of the increase in the outright purchase of the long-term JGBs.

[29] As a natural extension of our model, we also estimated the following GARCH-M-MA model.

$$r_t^s - r_t^f = \alpha h_t + \beta(CA_t) + \gamma(OP_t) + c + \sum_{i=0}^{k}\omega_i \varepsilon_{t+k-i}$$

$$\varepsilon_t \sim N(0, h_t^2), \quad h_t^2 = \gamma_e \varepsilon_{t-1}^2 + \beta_h(CA_t) + \gamma_h(OP_t) + c_h$$

Here, the conditional standard deviation influences the risk premium. However, since main results do not change, we do not report them.

Forward Exchange Risk Premium and Volatility

In the estimation of the forward exchange risk premium, we adopt the same methodology as that for stock returns, but also include the intervention by Japan's Ministry of Finance (INT_t) as an explanatory variable, following Ballie and Obsterberg (1997). Replacing the expected future spot rate $E_t[s_{t+k}]$ with the actual rate s_{t+k} in equation 18, we estimate the following model using GMM.[30]

$$s_{t+k} - f_{t,k} = \alpha(IV_t^e) + \beta(CA_t) + \gamma(OP_t) + \theta(INT_t) + c + \xi_t^e, \qquad (23)$$

where $\xi_t^e \equiv s_{t+k} - E_t[s_{t+k}]$ is a forecast error of spot rate.

Similarly, in order to examine the effect of the quantitative easing on the implied volatility of exchange rate, we also estimate the following regression.

$$IV_t^e = \rho_v(IV_{t-1}^e) + \beta_v CA_t + \gamma_v OP_t + \theta_v(INT_t) + c_v + \mu_t^e. \qquad (24)$$

The parameters of equations 23 and 24 are jointly estimated with GMM. To check the robustness of the results, we also estimate equation 23 and 24 with the alternative assumptions that ξ_t^e follows MA(k-1) and μ_t^e follows GARCH(1,1).

Credit Spreads and Volatilities of Corporate Bond Prices

For each grade of corporate bond (indexed by i) with credit spread CS_t^i at date t, we estimate the following equation:

$$CS_t^i = \phi_i(IR_t) + \alpha_i(HV_{t-1}^i) + \delta_i(IV_t^s) + \beta_i(CA_t) + \gamma_i(OP_t) + c_i + \xi_t^i. \qquad (25)$$

Two alternative volatility measures (HV_t^i and IV_t^s) and indicators of quantitative monetary easing (CA_t and OP_t) are used as explanatory variables. Previous studies use an interest rate (IR_t) as an explanatory variable for the expected default rate.[31] Here, we use yields on ten-year JGBs as a measure of IR_t.

---

[30] The risk premium can be different depending on the day of the week. The usual explanation for this phenomena is that volatility reflects volume of trading and also the flow of information to the market. Therefore, we also estimated equation 23 allowing for day of the week effects, but the main conclusion does not change at all. In order to conserve space, we do not report them.

[31] See the discussion above on page 15. As pointed out by Longstaff and Schwartz (1995), a decrease in the default-free rate implies a lower risk-neutral mean growth rate of assets, and, fixing the initial value of the firm and the default boundary for assets, risk-neutral survival probabilities go down, raising credit spreads (suggesting $\phi_i < 0$). Collin-Dufresne et al. (2001) argues that the expected default probability might increase and the expected recovery rate might decrease in times of recession when it is likely the case of a decrease in the long-term interest rates (also suggesting $\phi_i < 0$). On the other hand, as pointed by Duffie and Singleton (2003), if we take the firm's cash flow process as given and raise interest rates,

Collin-Dufresne, et al. (2001) suggest that the residuals from the regression for credit spreads are highly cross-correlated. In addition, the disturbances may be both heteroscedastic and/or auto-correlated. Therefore, we estimate the parameters of a system of equations, with one equation of the type of equation 25 for each CS_t^i, using GMM.[32]

In order to examine the effect of the quantitative easing on the volatilities of credit spreads, we estimate the following regression.

$$HV_t^i = \beta_{hv}^i CA_{t-k+1} + \gamma_{hv}^i OP_{t-k+1} + c^i + \mu_t^i,$$
(26)

$$\text{where } HV_t^i = \sqrt{\frac{1}{k}\sum_{j=0}^{k-1}\left[CS_{t-j}^i - \frac{1}{k}\sum_{j=0}^{k-1}CS_{t-j}^i\right]^2}$$

Taking into account the definition of historical volatility, it is reasonable to use the lagged variables of quantitative easing measures. Because the shocks to historical volatility HV_t^i are overlapping, the error term μ_t^i follows MA(k-1). We estimate equation 26 by GMM.

5. Estimation Results

5.1. Risk Premium on Stock Return

Tables 3 and 4 show the estimation results using GMM and the MA-GARCH model respectively. Although the estimates shown in Tables 3 and 4 differ across the estimation methods and sample periods, the main results are same.[33] (Recall that we have daily data on OP_t through June 30, 2003, whereas the daily data available for CA_t ends in March 31, 2004. In order to compare the effects of CA_t with those of OP_t, we also estimate the model with CA_t for the sub-sample period through June 30, 2003.)

---

then the entire path of the market value of the firm is lowered, thus advancing its default time and widening credit spreads (suggesting $\phi_i > 0$). But, using a VAR analysis, Duffie and Singleton (2003) found the negative correlation between credit spreads and interest rates, which is consistent with the views of Longstaff and Schwartz (1995) and Collin-Dufresne et al. (2001).

[32] We also estimate equation 25 with SUR. But, the main results do not change much.

[33] In order to check the sensitivity of our results to the sample period more rigorously, we conduct rolling regressions by changing the end of sample period by quarter. (The beginning of the sample period is fixed at January 21, 2000.) For the sake of brevity, we omit the results, but find that main conclusion does not change.

Both tables show that the parameter α (column 1) is positive and statistically significant in most cases, which means that an increase in the implied volatility leads to the increase in the risk premium on stocks. As in many previous studies, the parameter ρ_v (column 3) exceeds 0.9, which means that implied volatility is highly persistent. The parameters β_v and γ_v are negative, and the former is statistically significant. That is, an increase in current account balances has an indirect effect of decreasing the risk premium through an influence on the implied volatility of stock return.

The parameters β and γ (column 2), which measure the direct effect of portfolio rebalancing, are positive and statistically significant, consistent with our theory of quantitative easing. Moreover, the total effect of quantitative easing on risk premium, as calculated by equation 16, is positive. Therefore, our estimates indicate that quantitative easing, in as far as it affected stock prices through portfolio-rebalancing effects and by affecting volatility, caused the risk premium of stocks to increase.

5.2. Forward Exchange Risk Premium

Estimation results for the forward exchange risk premium are shown in Tables 5 and 6. As shown, inclusion of the intervention by Japan's Ministry of Finance as an independent variable does not change the main results. Both tables show: (1) An increase in the implied volatility of exchange rates leads to an increase in the forward exchange risk premium, i.e. $\alpha > 0$; (2) Implied volatility is highly persistent, i.e. $\rho_v > 0.9$; and (3) Quantitative easing reduces implied volatility; i.e. β_v, $\gamma_v < 0$, thereby, indirectly decreasing the forward exchange risk premium.

With regard to the direct effect of quantitative easing on the risk premium, as measured by the parameters β and γ, the results are mixed.[34] The estimation results based on GMM, shown in Table 5, indicates that the parameters β and γ are negative and statistically significant in most cases, which implies that the quantitative easing directly leads to a decrease in the forward exchange risk premium. On the other hand, the estimation results based on MA-GARCH model, shown in Table 6, indicate that the parameters β and γ are statistically insignificant. However, unlike the case of risk premium on stock returns, we can at least exclude the possibility that the quantitative

---

[34] More mixed and inconclusive results for the effect of intervention are obtained. For example, with regard to the indirect effect, the estimated parameter θ_v is statistically significant, but the sign differs between estimation methods.

easing has the adverse effect of raising the forward exchange risk premium. Rather, we may not reject the possibility that the quantitative easing directly reduces the forward exchange risk premium. This result may be related to the fact that the return on foreign currency asset is not pro-cyclical for domestic investors. As a whole, we may conclude that the quantitative easing has some decreasing effect on the forward exchange risk premium, taking into account the indirect effect also.

5.3. Credit Spreads

The estimation results for credit spreads are shown in Tables 7 - 9. Table 7 shows the results where the current accounts (CA_t) and the historical volatility (HV_t^i) are used as measures of quantitative easing and volatility, respectively.[35] Table 8 uses the outstanding balance of outright purchase (OP_t) of long-term JGB, and maintains the use of historical volatility (HV_t^i). Table 9 shows the results using current accounts (CA_t) balances, but switches to using the implied volatility of stock prices (IV_t^s).[36] All these specifications share three results:[37]

First, the parameters α_i (for historical volatility) and δ_i (for implied volatility) in the lower-grade corporate bonds (Baa) are statistically significant and positive. That is, an increase in the volatility leads to the increase in the credit spreads for lower-grade bonds. However, the parameters α_i and δ_i in higher-grade corporate bonds are statistically significant and positive in some cases, but negative in other cases. The negative values are consistent with our theory in the case where λ_1^j is sufficiently negative. Appendix (section A.3.2 (a)) shows that counter-cyclical assets with a sufficiently $\lambda_1^j < 0$ leads

---

[35] We estimate the model with a historical volatility of the credit spreads both over the past five business days and ten business days. Since the main results do not change, we only show the result based on the historical volatility over the past five business days.

[36] In Table 9, for the sake of brevity, we present the results only for the effect of the increase in the current accounts. We do not report the results for the effect of the increase in the outright purchase of long-term JGBs, since we find the almost same results as those for the effect of the increase in the current accounts.

[37] They also share a fourth result regarding the effect of the interest rate on the credit spreads. Unlike the previous empirical literature, we find that the sign of the parameter ϕ_i is positive and statistically significant in most cases. This is probably because of the commitment effect of the BOJ. During our sample period, the BOJ committed to continuing the quantitative easing until the inflation rate exceeds 0%. As this commitment effect permeated through the financial market, the long-term interest rates declined, which is expected to lead to the improvement of the economy. If this is the case, the decline in the long-term interest rates will reduce the expected default rate (and hence credit spreads).

to $\rho[r_t^m, r_t^j] < 0$. Then, when the correlation $\rho[r_t^m, r_t^j]$ is negative, the coefficient on the volatility measures in equation 13 and 14 becomes negative, as shown in page 11.[38]

Second, the direct effects of the quantitative easing on credit spreads are to reduce them for high-grade corporate-bonds but to increase them for low-grade corporate bonds. (The effect of the quantitative easing on the mid-grade, i.e. A-grade, corporate bond's spreads depends on the sample period.) In particular, the parameter β_i for high-grade corporate bond spreads is negative and statistically significant, although the increase in current accounts by 10 trillion yen reduces credit spreads for Aa-grade corporate bonds only by 1 - 4 basis points. The parameter γ_i for high-grade corporate bond's spreads is also negative and statistically significant, and the increase in the outstanding of outright purchase of JGBs by 10 trillion yen reduces credit spreads for Aa-grade corporate bonds by 6 - 8 basis points. But for low-grade corporate-bond spreads, the parameters β_i and γ_i are positive and statistically significant in most cases.[39] An increase in current accounts by 10 trillion yen increases credit spreads for Baa-grade corporate bonds by 1- 24 basis points. An increase in the outstanding of outright purchase of JGBs by 10 trillion yen increases credit spreads for Baa-grade corporate bonds by 21 - 44 basis points.

Finally, we also find that the effects of the quantitative easing on volatility differ according to the grade of the corporate bond. Table 10 shows that the parameters β_{hv}^i and γ_{hv}^i for high-grade corporate bonds' volatilities tend to be negative and statistically significant. That is, quantitative easing reduces the high-grade corporate bonds' volatility. But quantitative easing does not have such an effect on the volatility of low-grade corporate bonds.[40] Table 10 also shows that this result does not depend on the day-length (k) of historical volatilities.[41]

---

[38] Because of the pro-cyclicality of market portfolio, an increase in the volatility of counter-cyclical asset prices leads to a decrease in the investors' exposures to business cycle risk. This results in a decrease in the risk premium of the counter-cyclical asset.

[39] Since credit spreads show evidence of substantial persistence over time, it may not be sufficient to know the contemporaneous correlations among spreads, quantitative easing measures, and other variables. Following Duffie and Singleton (2003), in order to explore the dynamic correlations among spreads and other variables, we estimate the impulse response functions by using a VAR. The impulse response functions suggest that our main conclusion is robust. That is, an increase in current accounts leads to a statistical significant and prolonged increase in the low-grade corporate bonds' spreads.

[40] We must note that the effects of quantitative easing on the decrease in the high-grade corporate bond's volatility do not necessarily contribute to the decrease in their credit spreads. This is because the parameter α_i in equation 25 is negative in some cases. However, the total effects of quantitative easing on

6. Some Further Considerations

This section discusses the robustness of our results with respect to three issues: (1) potential spurious regression, (2) cross-sectional differences in the measures of asset returns other than business-cycle risk, and (3) the endogeneity of monetary policy.

Spurious Regression

After the adoption of quantitative monetary easing (March 19, 2001), the BOJ monotonically increased the outstanding volume of current account balances by stages. Therefore, current account balances have an upward trend. If the independent variables also have a trend, which is unlikely in the case of stock return and forward exchange premium but likely in the case of credit spreads (Figure 4), the empirical estimates may suffer from the problem of spurious regression.

In order to address this issue, the model was reestimated with current account balances detrended (by linear trend), although we think that the concept of the detrended current accounts is vague from a theoretical view point and far from the concept of portfolio shares. For the sake of brevity, those estimation results are not reported but our main conclusion does not change. That is, an increase in the current accounts leads to an increase in the risk premium for stock returns and an increase in the credit spreads for low-grade corporate bonds.

Cross-Sectional Differences in the Measures of Asset Returns

The estimation strategy that we employ to detect portfolio-rebalancing effects is based on the excess returns of the different assets having different covariances with business-cycle. But those measured returns also differ in two other aspects: the maturities of the expected returns and whether the measured returns are derived from ex-ante forward-

---

high-grade corporate bond's credit spreads, measured by equation 16, are negative. Therefore, we can conclude that the quantitative easing has reduced credit spreads (and probably risk premium) for the high-grade corporate bonds.

[41] As noted earlier, the BOJ's quantitative easing has lowered the long-term JGB's rate and kept it stably lower. As our estimates indicate, this led to a decrease in the volatility of the yield on high-grade corporate bonds, which are relatively close substitutes for JGBs. However, our estimates do not indicate a reduction in the volatility of the yield on the low-grade corporate bonds with long maturities, probably because such bonds are not close substitutes for JGBs. Indeed, such an interpretation is consistent with the previous literature, which suggests: (1) high-grade bonds behave like Treasury bonds, but (2) low-grade bonds are more sensitive to stock returns. See Keim and Stambarugh (1986), Fama and French (1993), and Campbell and Ammer (1993), Kwan (1996), Blume, Keim and Patel (1991).

looking asset prices or proxied by ex-post returns. So it is possible these other cross-sectional differences are driving our results.

Although there are four possible combinations of returns being of long- or short-maturity and being ex-post or ex-ante, our measured returns fall into only two combinations. (See Table 11.) Both stock and foreign exchange returns are based on a rather short 22-day maturity and on ex-post returns, while both high- and low-grade corporate bond rates are based on rather long 1- to 5-year maturities and on ex-ante rate spreads. In each of the two combinations, one asset return exhibits an increase in response to quantitative easing while the other exhibits no increase or a decrease. Accordingly, these two characteristics (the maturity of the expected return and whether the measured return is based on forward-looking asset prices or ex-post returns) do not seem to be driving our results.

Endogeneity Problem

We found statistically significant effects of quantitative easing on risk premiums. However, if the BOJ raised the target balance for current accounts (or its outright purchases of long-term JGBs) in order to offset increases in risk premiums, there would be a positive correlation between measures of quantitative easing and error terms in equations 19, 23 and 25 - - inducing an upward bias to the estimated coefficient on quantitative easing. This raises the issue of whether quantitative easing is truly an exogenous signal or not.

We address this issue by using GMM, an instrumental variables method. As instrument variables, we used lagged variables (from one business day to three business days) of independent and dependent variables. The details of the choice of instrument variables are noted in each table. For example, in the estimation of equation 25, the use of the long-term government bond rate as an instrument variable avoids the estimation bias because the long-term government bond rate is uncorrelated with the error terms but correlated with measures of quantitative easing.

However, the BOJ may have private information on the future development of financial asset prices and may have responded to these expected future prices. If so, the forecast errors ξ_t^s and ξ_t^e in equations 19 and 23 may not be orthogonal to the lagged quantitative easing measures ($CA_{t-k}, OP_{t-k}, k = 1, 2, 3$). This may be particularly relevant when the forecast errors are auto-correlated. In order to address this potential problem, we reestimated equation 19, and 23 using the quantitative easing measures lagged by twenty-two to twenty-four business days (CA_{t-k} , OP_{t-k} , $k = 22, 23, 24$) as the instrument variables. Such one-month-before quantitative easing measures are unlikely be correlated with the forecast errors ξ_t^s and ξ_t^e . For the sake of brevity, we do not report the estimation results, but note that our main conclusions are not much affected by this change in the instrument variables.

Another potential problem is that our empirical results for credit spreads may reflect that both the BOJ's quantitative easing and credit spreads respond to a common factor. Indeed, as shown in Figure 7, credit spreads of low-grade corporate bonds seem to be correlated with the business cycle, to which the BOJ's quantitative easing presumably also responds. However, we obtained the results that quantitative easing increases risk premium not only for low-grade corporate bonds, but also for equities. (See Table 11.) As shown in Figure 7, the excess return for equities does not seem to be correlated with the business cycle. Accordingly, these cross-sectional results suggest that an endogenous policy response does not derive our result.

7. Summary and Conclusions

In the context of the Bank of Japan's policy of quantitative easing, we have explicitly considered portfolio-rebalancing effects and how they may be affected by the attempts of portfolio holders to diversify business-cycle risk. In this framework, an outright purchase of long-term government bonds does not necessarily reduce the portfolio risk of financial institutions and other private-sector investors and thereby generate room for new risk taking - - as has been suggested. Indeed, the portfolio risk associated with the business cycle may have increased as the BOJ's purchases of long-term government debt reduced the private-sector's holding of this asset whose returns are counter-cyclical,

If we focus only on the portfolio-rebalancing effects, and neglect the other effects such as the BOJ using quantitative easing to demonstrate resolve to keep short-term rates low, the BOJ's quantitative easing may have increased the demand for those JGB substitutes whose returns also are counter-cyclical. But these policy actions may have decreased the demand for assets whose returns are pro-cyclical and thus may have increased the risk premium for pro-cyclical assets. The following chart summarizes these estimation results.

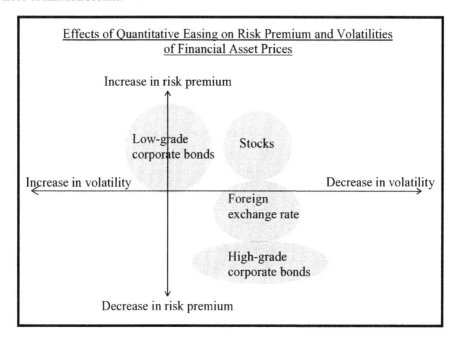

The shaded regions show the general ranges for the estimates of the effects of the quantitative easing on risk premiums (β and γ, on the vertical axis) and on volatility (β_v and γ_v, on the horizontal axis). For excess returns of high-grade corporate bonds, which presumably behave much like government bonds, quantitative easing had the standard effect of reducing risk premiums. And quantitative easing also had some effect of decreasing the forward exchange risk premium. On the other hand, the potential adverse effects of the quantitative easing were found in the markets for stocks and low-grade corporate bonds. In those markets, quantitative easing seems to have increased risk premiums.

Needless to say, these estimates capture only some of the effects of the BOJ's policy of quantitative easing and do not imply that the complete set of effects were adverse on net for Japan's economy. As to the most evident effects, the abundant and flexible provision of liquidity under the quantitative easing framework successfully maintained extremely easy monetary conditions and assuaged market participants' concerns over liquidity financing, thereby preserving financial market stability. The results that the quantitative easing lowers volatilities of the broad financial asset prices (except low-grade corporate bond prices) support this route. See the horizontal axis of the above chart.

However, clearly our analysis based on CAPM counsels caution in accepting the view that a massive large-scale purchase of JGBs by the Bank at the zero bound unambiguously provides benefits to financial markets. Although the dramatic increase in the outright purchases of long-term government bonds may be useful in demonstrating resolve to fight deflation, a central bank could note that there is a potential adverse side effect of such purchases. Accordingly, one of the safest conclusions is that such purchases should be used only to supplement the commitment effects, such as an attempt to influence expectations of future short rates.

Our analysis also suggests that complementing such open market purchases with other policies could mitigate the potential adverse side effects of quantitative easing. One such policy is to strengthen the capital position of financial institutions, which often has been pointed out by the BOJ. In terms of our model, a strengthened capital position might make a financial institution less adverse to business-cycle risk. Another possible prescription may be to broaden the range of assets that the BOJ purchases. Although their purchases do not fall directly within the province of monetary policy, the BOJ started purchasing stocks held by private banks in November 2002, with a view to further reducing the market risk pertaining to these stocks.[42] In June 2003, the BOJ also started purchasing asset-backed securities (ABSs), including asset-backed commercial paper, mainly backed by those assets related to small and medium-sized firms.[43] These measures have the potential to reduce the adverse side-effects of the quantitative easing and to strengthen the transmission mechanism of monetary policy in order to ensure that the beneficial effects of the quantitative easing permeate the economy.

---

[42] See Bank of Japan (2002a,b).

[43] See Bank of Japan (2003b).

Appendix

A1. Derivation of equations 11 and 12.

As seen in equation A1, $Cov[r_t^j, r_t^m]$ is affected by $\lambda_{1,m}$.

$$
\begin{aligned}
Cov[r_t^j, r_t^m] &= Cov[\lambda_0^j + \lambda_1^j Z_t + \varepsilon_t^j, \lambda_{0,m} + \lambda_{1,m} Z_t + \varepsilon_{t,m}] \\
&= Cov[\lambda_1^j Z_t, \lambda_{1,m} Z_t] + Cov[\lambda_1^j Z_t, \varepsilon_{t,m}] + Cov[\varepsilon_t^j, \lambda_{1,m} Z_t] + Cov[\varepsilon_t^j, \varepsilon_{t,m}] \quad (A1) \\
&= \lambda_1^j \lambda_{1,m} Var[Z_t] + w_j Var[\varepsilon_t^j]
\end{aligned}
$$

In turn, changes in the portfolio weight w_N affect $\lambda_{1,m}$ and thereby also $Cov[r_t^j, r_t^m]$.

$$
j = N, \quad \frac{\partial Cov[r_t^N, r_t^m]}{\partial w_N} = (\lambda_1^N \lambda_1^N + \lambda_{1,m}) Var[Z_t] + Var[\varepsilon_t^N] > 0 \tag{A2}
$$

$$
\forall j \neq N, \quad \frac{\partial Cov[r_t^j, r_t^m]}{\partial w_N} = \lambda_1^j \lambda_1^N Var[Z_t] \gtreqless 0 \;\; as \;\; \lambda_1^j \lesseqgtr 0 \tag{A3}
$$

For example, a decrease in w_N makes the market portfolio more pro-cyclical by increasing $\lambda_{1,m}$. This can be seen directly from our expression for r_t^m in equation 8, the definition $\lambda_{1,m} = \sum_{j=1}^N w_j \lambda_1^j$, and the assumption that $\lambda_1^N < 0$. The increase in the pro-cyclical behavior of r_t^m increases the covariance of r_t^m with other pro-cyclical assets ($\lambda_1^j > 0$), and decreases the covariance of r_t^m with counter-cyclical assets ($\lambda_1^j < 0$).

A2. Derivation of the conditions stated in the text immediately following equation 13.

To repeat, equation 13 is:

$$
E[r_t^j - r_t^f] \cong A_0^j + A_1^j \rho[r_t^m, r_t^j]^\Delta + A_2^j \sqrt{Var[r_t^j]}^\Delta + A_3^j \sqrt{Var[r_t^m]}^\Delta \tag{A4}
$$

Letting the subscript " * " indicate the value around which the Taylor approximation is taken and assuming $E[r_t^j - r_t^f] > 0$, the coefficients in equation 13 are:

$$
A_0^j = \left(\kappa \rho[r_t^m, r_t^j] \sqrt{Var[r_t^j]} \sqrt{Var[r_t^m]} \right)_* \tag{A5}
$$

$$
A_1^j = \left(\kappa \sqrt{Var[r_t^j]} \sqrt{Var[r_t^m]} \right)_* > 0 \tag{A6}
$$

$$
A_2^j = \left(\kappa \rho[r_t^m, r_t^j] \sqrt{Var[r_t^m]} \right)_* \tag{A7}
$$

$$A_3^j = \left(\kappa \rho[r_t^m, r_t^j] \sqrt{Var[r_t^j]} \right)_*$$ (A8)

These equations imply the conditions stated in the text immediately following equation 13.

A3. Derivation of the sign of β_{QE}^j in equation 14.

Noting that increases in quantitative easing (an open market purchases of government bonds) decrease the share of government bond in the market portfolio (w_N) and using equation 13, we have

$$\beta_{QE}^j \equiv \frac{\partial E[r_t^j - r_t^f]}{\partial QE} = -\left(\frac{\partial E[r_t^j - r_t^f]}{\partial w_N} \right) = -\left(A_1^j \frac{\partial \rho[r_t^m, r_t^j]}{\partial w_N} + A_3^j \frac{\partial \sqrt{Var[r_t^m]}}{\partial w_N} \right).$$ (A9)

As equation A9 shows, there are two portfolio-rebalancing effects. One is the effect on the degree of linear movements of r_t^j and r_t^m and the second is the effect on the amount of uncertainty in financial markets as measured by $\sqrt{Var[r_t^m]}$.

A3.1. Sign of $A_1^j \partial \rho[r_t^m, r_t^j]/\partial w_N$

(a) $A_1^j > 0$, from equation A6.

(b) Need sign of $\partial \rho[r_t^m, r_t^j]/\partial w_N$.

Because in equation 13 we are considering the change in $\rho[r_t^m, r_t^j]$ for given values of $\sqrt{Var[r_t^m]}$ and $\sqrt{Var[r_t^j]}$, the sign of $\partial \rho[r_t^m, r_t^j]/\partial w_N$ is the same as the sign of $\partial Cov[r_t^m, r_t^N]/\partial w_N$, which is given by equations A2 and A3. Thus,

    i. $\dfrac{\partial \rho[r_t^m, r_t^j]}{\partial w_N} > 0$ *for* $\lambda_1^j < 0$, *given* $\sqrt{Var[r_t^m]}$ *and* $\sqrt{Var[r_t^j]}$

    ii. $\dfrac{\partial \rho[r_t^m, r_t^j]}{\partial w_N} < 0$ *for* $\lambda_1^j > 0$, *given* $\sqrt{Var[r_t^m]}$ *and* $\sqrt{Var[r_t^j]}$

(c) Thus, the sign of $A_1^j \partial \rho[r_t^m, r_t^j]/\partial w_N$ will be

    i. positive for $\lambda_1^j < 0$

    ii. negative for $\lambda_1^j > 0$,

30

(d) This is one "portfolio-rebalancing" effect, i.e. the change in the portfolio weight can affect the degree of linear relation.

A3.2. Sign of $A_3^j \, \partial \sqrt{Var[r_t^m]}/\partial w_N$

(a) Need sign of $A_3^j = $ sign of $\rho[r_t^m, r_t^j]$

$$
\begin{aligned}
\rho[r_t^m, r_t^j] &= \frac{Cov[r_t^m, r_t^j]}{\sqrt{Var[r_t^m]}\sqrt{Var[r_t^j]}} \\
&= \lambda_1^j \lambda_{1,m} \frac{Var[Z_t]}{\sqrt{Var[r_t^m]}\sqrt{Var[r_t^j]}} + w_j \frac{Var[\varepsilon_t^j]}{\sqrt{Var[r_t^m]}\sqrt{Var[r_t^j]}}
\end{aligned}
$$

using equation A1. Thus,

i. $A_3^j > 0$ and $\rho[r_t^m, r_t^j] > 0$ for an asset with $\lambda_1^j > 0$

ii. $A_3^j < 0$ and $\rho[r_t^m, r_t^j] < 0$ for an asset with a sufficiently $\lambda_1^j < 0$.

(b) Need sign of $\partial \sqrt{Var[r_t^m]}/\partial w_N$

This was discussed above following equation 10 and again is part of our "alternative" story on page 11.

$$
\frac{\partial Var[r_t^m]}{\partial w_N} = 2\lambda_{1,m} \lambda_1^N Var[Z_t] + 2w_N Var[\varepsilon_t^N] \gtrless 0 \tag{A10}
$$

(c) Thus the sign of $A_3^j \, \partial \sqrt{Var[r_t^m]}/\partial w_N$ may be positive or negative.

But the interesting point is that it need not be positive, which would imply that this effect through $Var[r_t^m]$ would decrease excess returns -- as discussed above in the quote on page 5. It is possible that the risk in the market would increase ($\partial \sqrt{Var[r_t^m]}/\partial w_N < 0$) and that $A_3^j > 0$ for some assets, implying that an increase in open market operations could increase risk premiums on those assets with $\lambda_1^j > 0$, meaning that the sign of $A_3^j \, \partial \sqrt{Var[r_t^m]}/\partial w_N$ is negative.

A3.3. Pulling it all together, what is the sign of β_{QE}^j in equation 14?

$$
\beta_{QE}^j = -\left(A_1^j \frac{\partial \rho[r_t^m, r_t^j]}{\partial w_N} + A_3^j \frac{\partial \sqrt{Var[r_t^m]}}{\partial w_N} \right) \tag{A9}
$$

(a) Thus both terms inside the bracket will tend to be negative the more positive is λ_1^j and the more negative is λ_1^N, for a given value of $\lambda_{1,m} > 0$.

(b) If both terms are negative, then $\beta_{QE}^j > 0$ and an increase in quantitative easing will increase the excess return on asset j.

References

Andrés, Javier, David López-Salido and Edward Nelson (2004), "Tobin's Imperfect Asset Substitution in Optimizing General Equilibrium," The Federal Reserve Bank of St. Louis, Working Paper 2004-003A.

Auerbach and Obstfeld (2004), "The Case for Open-Market Purchase in a Liquidity Trap," available at http://emlab.berkeley.edu/users/auerbach/zerotrap24.pdf.

Cochrane, John H. (2001), *Asset Pricing*, Princeton University Press (Princeton, NJ).

Baillie, Richard T. and William P. Obsterberg (1997), "Central Bank Intervention and Risk in the Forward Market," *Journal of International Economics*, Vol. 43, pp.483-497.

Bank of Japan (2002a), "New Initiative Toward Financial System Stability," September 2003.

Bank of Japan (2002b), "Stock Purchase Guidelines," November 2003.

Bank of Japan (2003a), "Outlook and Risk Assessment of the Economy and Prices," April 2003.

Bank of Japan (2003b), "Purchases of Asset-Backed Securities," April 2003.

Bernanke, Ben S. (2000), "Japanese Monetary Policy: A Case of Self-Induced Paralysis?," for presentation at the ASSA meetings, Boston MA, January 9, 2000.

Bernanke, Ben S. and Vincent R. Reinhart (2004), "Conducting Monetary Policy at Very Low Short-Term Interest Rates," Presented at the International Center for Monetary and Banking Studies Lecture, Geneva, Switzerland, January 14, 2004.

Blume, Marshall E., Donald B. Keim, and Sandeep A. Patel (1991), "Returns and Volatility of Low-grade Bonds: 1977-1989," *Journal of Finance*, Vol.46, pp.49-74.

Brunner, Karl and Allan H. Meltzer (1976), "An Aggregative Theory for a Closed Economy," in Jerome L. Stein, ed., *Monetarism*, North Holland, Amsterdam, pp. 69-103.

Campbell, John Y, and John, Ammer (1993), "What Moves the Stock and Bond Markets? A Variance Decomposition for Long-Term Asset Returns," *Journal of Finance*, Vol. 48, Issue.1, pp. 3-37.

Clouse, James, Dale Henderson, Athanasios Orphanides, David Small, and Peter Tinsley (2000), "Monetary Policy When the Nominal Short-Term Interest Rate Is Zero," Finance and Economics Discussion Series, No. 2000-51, Board of Governors of the Federal Reserve System.

Collin-Dufresne, Pierre, Robert S. Goldstein, and J. Spencer Martin. (2001), "The Determinants of Credit Spread Changes," *Journal of Finance*, Vol. LVI, No.6, pp.2177-2207.

Duffie, Darrell, and Kenneth J. Singleton. (2003), *Credit Risk – Pricing, Measurement, and Management*, Princeton University Press.

Elton, Edwin J. (1999), "Expected Return, Realized return, and Asset Pricing Tests," *Journal of Finance*, Vo.54, pp.1199-1221.

Elton, Edwin J., Martin J. Gruber, Deepak Agrawal, and Chistopher Mann (2001), "Explaining the Rate Spread on Corporate Bonds," *Journal of Finance*, Vol. LVI, No.1, pp.247-277.

Eggertsson, Gauti B. and Michael Woodford (2003), "The Zero Bound on Interest Rates and Optimal Monetary Policy," *Brookings Papers on Economic Activity*, Vol.0, issue.1, pp. 139-211.

Fama, Eugene F. and Kenneth R. French (1993), "Common Risk Factors in the Returns on Stock and Bonds," *Journal of Financial Economics*, Vol.33, pp.3-56.

Frankel, Jefferey A. (1985), "Portfolio Shares as Beta Breakers," *Journal of Portfolio Management*, Vol. 11, No.5, pp.18-23.

Fukui, Toshihiko (2003), "Challenges for Monetary Policy in Japan," Speech at the Spring Meeting of the Japan Society of Monetary Economics, on the occasion of its 60th anniversary, on June 1 2003.

Keim, Donald B., and Robert F. Stambarugh (1986), "Predicting returns in the Stock and Bond markets," *Journal of Financial Economics*, Vol.17. pp.357-390.

Kimura, Takeshi, Hiroshi Kobayashi, Jun Muranaga, and Hiroshi Ugai, (2003*)*, "The effect of the increase in the monetary base on Japan's economy at zero interest rates: an empirical analysis," in *Monetary policy in a changing environment*, BIS papers, No.19., pp.276-312.

King, Marvin (1999), "Challenges for monetary policy: new and old", in Federal Reserve Bank of Kansas City, *New challenges for monetary policy.*

King, Marvin (2002), "No money, no inflation: the role of money in the economy", *Bank of England Quarterly Bulletin*, Summer 2002.

Krugman Paul (2000), "Thinking about the Liquidity Trap*," Journal of the Japanese and International Economies*, Vol.14, Iss.4, pp. 221-37.

Kwan, Simon H.(1996), "Firm-Specific Information and the Correlation between Individual Stocks and Bonds," *Journal of Financial Economics*, Vol.40, pp.63-80.

Lintner, John. (1969), "The Aggregation of Investor's Diverse Judgments and Preferences in Purely Competitive Security Markets," *Journal of Financial and Quantitative Analysis*, Vol.4, No.4, pp.347-400.

Lintner, John. (1970), "The Market Price of Risk, Size of Market and Investor's Risk Aversion," *Review of Economics and Statistics*, Vol.52, No.1, pp.87-99.

Longstaff, Francis A., and Eduardo Schwartz (1995), "A Simple Approach to Valuing Risky Fixed and Floating Rate Debt," *Journal of Finance*, Vol.50, pp.789-821.

Meltzer, Allan. (1999), "The Transmission Process," March 1999. Manuscript, Carnegie Mellon University and the American Enterprise Institute.

Muto, Toshiro (2003), "Structural Changes in the World Economy and Challenges Facing Japan's Economy," Speech at the JCIF International Finance Seminar, on June 17, 2003.

Oda, Nobuyuki, and Kunio, Okina (2001), "Further Monetary Easing Policies under the Non-negativity Constraints of Nominal Interest Rates: Summary of the Discussion Based on Japan's Experience," *Monetary and Economic Studies*, Vol. 19, pp. 323-60.

Okina Kunio, and Shigenori Shiratsuka (2003), "Policy Commitment and Expectation Formations: Japan's Experience under Zero Interest Rates," IMES Discussion Paper Series, Bank of Japan , No.2003-E-5..

Roley, Vance V. (1979), "A Theory of Federal Debt Management," *American Economic Review*, Vol. 69, Issue 5, pp.915-926.

Shirakawa Masaaki (2002), "One year under 'quantitative easing'," IMES Discussion Paper Series, Bank of Japan, No. 2002-E-3.

Okina Kunio, and Shigenori Shiratsuka (2003), "Policy Commitment and Expectation Formations: Japan's Experience under Zero Interest Rates," IMES Discussion Paper Series, Bank of Japan , No. 2003-E-5..

Tobin, James (1963), "An Essay on the Principles of Debt Management," Fiscal and Debt Management Policies, Commission on Money and Credit.

Tobin, James (1969), "A General Equilibrium Approach to Monetary Theory," *Journal of Money, Credit, and Banking*, 1:1, pp. 15-29.

Tobin, James (1982), "Money and Finance in the Macroeconomic Process," Journal of Money, Credit and Banking, Vol. 14, pp. 171-203.

(Table1)

Development of Monetary Easing

Date	Target balance of current accounts (tril.yen)	Outright purchase of long-term JGBs (bil.yen/month)
Mar. 2001	Around 5	400
Aug. 2001	Around 6	600
Sep. 2001	Above 6	↓
Dec. 2001	Around 10-15	800
Feb. 2002	↓	1000
Oct. 2002	Around 15-20	1200
Apr. 2003	Around 17-22	↓
Apr. 2003	Around 22-27	↓
May. 2003	Around 27-30	↓
Oct. 2003	Around 27-32	↓
Jan. 2004	Around 30-35	↓

(Through March 2004)

(Table2)

Basic Structure of BOJ's Balance Sheet
(at the end of June 2003)

Assets	Liabilities and Capital
Long-term JGBs (60.4)	Banknotes (71.2)
Short-term market operations (46.6)	Current account (28.9)
Underwritten TB/FB (9.7)	Government deposit & others (19.9)
Others (8.6)	Capital (5.3)

(Unit: trillion yen)

(Table3)

Risk Premium and Volatility of Stock Prices (1)

— Estimation based on GMM —

$$r_t^s - r_t^f = \alpha(IV_t^s) + \beta(CA_t) + \gamma(OP_t) + c + \xi_t^s \tag{19}$$

$$IV_t^s = \rho_v(IV_{t-1}^s) + \beta_v CA_t + \gamma_v OP_t + c_v + \mu_t^s \tag{21}$$

(1) Effects of an Increase in the Outstanding Balance of Current Account Deposits ($\gamma = \gamma_v = 0$)

Sample period	α	β	ρ_v	β_v	J-statistic Eq(19) S.E.	Eq(21) S.E.
2001/1/21 ~ 2003/6/30	2.010** (0.999)	3.501*** (1.170)	0.929*** (0.009)	-0.010** (0.004)	0.0155 S.E.=74.27	S.E.=2.19
2001/1/21 ~ 2004/3/31	1.265 (1.104)	3.093*** (0.720)	0.922*** (0.010)	-0.010** (0.004)	0.0131 S.E.=73.31	S.E.=2.11

(2) Effects of an Increase in the Outstanding Balance of Outright Purchase of Long-term JGB ($\beta = \beta_v = 0$)

Sample period	α	γ	ρ_v	γ_v	J-statistic Eq(19) S.E.	Eq(21) S.E.
2001/1/21 ~ 2003/6/30	1.811* (0.977)	3.317** (1.629)	0.928*** (0.009)	-0.003 (0.059)	0.0144 S.E.=75.74	S.E.=2.19

(Note1) Numbers in parentheses are standard errors. ***/**/* denotes significance at the 1/5/10 percent level.

(Note 2) Instrumental variables of GMM;

Eq.(19)   constant term, $r_{t-k-j}^s - r_{t-k-j}^f, IV_{t-j}^s, CA_{t-j}$ or OP_{t-j} ($j=1,2,3$)

Eq.(21)   constant term, IV_{t-j}^s, CA_{t-j} or OP_{t-j} ($j=1,2,3$)

(Note 3) Based on Hansen test, we do not statistically reject the overidentifying restrictions (at the 20% significance level) for each estimation.

(Note4) ▢ indicates the effect of quantitative easing is statistically significant and effective. ▨ indicates the effect of quantitative easing is statistically significant but harmful.

(Table 4)

Risk Premium and Volatility of Stock Prices (2)
—— Estimation based on MA-GARCH Model ——

$$r_t^s - r_t^f = \alpha(IV_t^s) + \beta(CA_t) + \gamma(OP_t) + c + \sum_{i=0}^{k} \omega_i \varepsilon_{t+k-i} \tag{22}$$

$$IV_t^s = \rho_v(IV_{t-1}^s) + \beta_v CA_t + \gamma_v OP_t + c_v + \mu_t^s \tag{21}$$

$$\mu_t^s \sim N(0, h_t^2), \quad h_t^2 = \lambda_\varepsilon \varepsilon_{t-1}^2 + \lambda_h h_{t-1}^2$$

(1) Effects of an Increase in the Outstanding Balance of Current Account Deposits ($\gamma = \gamma_v = 0$)

Sample period	α	β	ρ_v	β_v	Eq.(22)		Eq.(21)	
					$Adj.R^2$	S.E.	$Adj.R^2$	S.E.
2001/1/21 ~ 2003/6/30	1.370*** (0.240)	2.076*** (0.549)	0.893*** (0.016)	-0.063*** (0.021)	0.926	21.24	0.886	2.06
2001/1/21 ~ 2004/3/31	1.133*** (0.235)	2.097*** (0.470)	0.905*** (0.014)	-0.047** (0.018)	0.927	21.23	0.885	1.94

(2) Effects of an Increase in the Outstanding Balance of Outright Purchase of Long-term JGB
($\beta = \beta_v = 0$)

Sample period	α	γ	ρ_v	γ_v	Eq.(22)		Eq.(21)	
					$Adj.R^2$	S.E.	$Adj.R^2$	S.E.
2001/1/21 ~ 2003/6/30	0.977*** (0.138)	3.622*** (1.296)	0.914*** (0.014)	-0.015 (0.019)	0.931	20.49	0.883	1.95

(Note1) Numbers in parentheses are standard errors. ***/**/* denotes significance at the 1/5/10 percent level.

(Note2) ☐ indicates the effect of quantitative easing is statistically significant and effective.
▨ indicates the effect of quantitative easing is statistically significant but harmful.

(Table 5)

Risk Premium and Volatility of Exchange Rate (1)
—— Estimation based on GMM ——

$$s_{t+k} - f_{t,k} = \alpha(IV_t^e) + \beta(CA_t) + \gamma(OP_t) + \theta(INT_t) + c + \xi_t^e \tag{23}$$

$$IV_t^e = \rho_v(IV_{t-1}^e) + \beta_v CA_t + \gamma_v OP_t + \theta_v(INT_t) + c_v + \mu_t^e \tag{24}$$

(1) Effects of an Increase in the Outstanding Balance of Current Account Deposits ($\gamma = \gamma_v = 0$)

Sample period	α	β	θ	ρ_v	β_v	θ_v	J-statistic Eq.(23) S.E.	Eq.(24) S.E.
2001/1/21 ~ 2003/6/30	2.971* (1.746)	-0.781** (0.393)	—	0.932*** (0.007)	-0.006*** (0.002)	—	0.010 S.E.=31.14	S.E.=0.455
	1.103 (1.920)	-1.016*** (0.392)	0.085*** (0.023)	0.935*** (0.009)	-0.005** (0.002)	-0.0002 (0.0003)	0.016 S.E.=31.74	S.E.=0.463
2001/1/21 ~ 2004/3/31	2.751* (1.404)	-0.696** (0.323)	—	0.937*** (0.006)	-0.003** (0.002)	—	0.006 S.E.=31.18	S.E.=0.490
	1.936 (1.533)	-0.759*** (0.299)	0.036*** (0.016)	0.941*** (0.009)	-0.0007 (0.002)	-0.0006** (0.001)	0.007 S.E.=31.73	S.E.=0.488

(2) Effects of an Increase in the Outstanding Balance of Outright Purchase of Long-term JGB ($\beta = \beta_v = 0$)

Sample period	α	γ	θ	ρ_v	γ_v	θ_v	J-statistic Eq.(23) S.E.	Eq.(24) S.E.
2001/1/21 ~ 2003/6/30	4.089** (2.016)	-0.689 (0.608)	—	0.941*** (0.006)	-0.007** (0.002)	—	0.0069 S.E.=31.73	S.E.=0.455
	1.863 (2.048)	-1.022** (0.519)	0.004 (0.003)	0.951*** (0.015)	-0.004 (0.003)	-0.0001* (0.00006)	0.011 S.E.=31.73	S.E.=0.507

(Note1) Numbers in parentheses are standard errors. ***/**/* denotes significance at the 1/5/10 percent level.

(Note2) Instrumental variables of GMM;

Eq.(23) constant term, $s_{t-j} - f_{t-k-j,k}$, IV_{t-j}^e, CA_{t-j} or OP_{t-j} $(j = 1,2,3)$

Eq.(24) constant term, IV_{t-j}^e, CA_{t-j} or OP_{t-j} $(j = 1,2,3)$

When INT_t is included as an explanatory variable in Eq.(23) and (24), INT_{t-j} ($j = 1,2,3$) are also used as instrumental variables.

(Note3) Based on Hansen test, we do not statistically reject the overidentifying restrictions (at the 20% significance level) for each estimation.

(Note4) □ indicates the effect of quantitative easing is statistically significant and effective.

(Table 6)

Risk Premium and Volatility of Exchange Rate (2)
—— Estimation based on MA-GARCH Model ——

$$s_{t+k} - f_{t,k} = \alpha(IV_t^e) + \beta(CA_t) + \gamma(OP_t) + \theta(INT_t) + c + + \sum_{i=0}^{k} \omega_i \varepsilon_{t+k-i} \quad (23)$$

$$IV_t^e = \rho_v(IV_{t-1}^e) + \beta_v CA_t + \gamma_v OP_t + \theta_v(INT_t) + c_v + \mu_t^e \quad (24)$$

$$\mu_i^e \sim N(0, h_t^2), \quad h_t^2 = \lambda_c \varepsilon_{t-1}^2 + \lambda_h h_{t-1}^2$$

(1) Effects of an Increase in the Outstanding Balance of Current Account Deposits ($\gamma = \gamma_v = 0$)

Sample period	α	β	θ	ρ_v	β_v	θ_v	Eq.(23) Adj.R^2	Eq.(23) S.E.	Eq.(24) Adj.R^2	Eq.(24) S.E.
2001/1/21 ~ 2003/6/30	1.869*** (0.412)	0.010 (0.226)	---	0.939*** (0.009)	-0.005*** (0.002)	---	0.937	8.075	0.903	0.456
	1.921*** (0.535)	-0.155 (0.260)	-0.00005 (0.0001)	0.940*** (0.013)	-0.006*** (0.002)	0.0008* (0.0002)	0.925	8.843	0.909	0.442
2001/1/21 ~ 2004/3/31	1.380*** (0.328)	-0.282 (0.179)	---	0.936*** (0.019)	-0.004* (0.002)	---	0.941	7.964	0.895	0.489
	1.445*** (0.335)	-0.221 (0.193)	0.00003 (0.00008)	0.935*** (0.014)	-0.006*** (0.002)	0.0003** (0.0001)	0.944	7.704	0.896	0.487

(2) Effects of an Increase in the Outstanding Balance of Outright Purchase of Long-term JGB
($\beta = \beta_v = 0$)

Sample period	α	γ	θ	ρ_v	γ_v	θ_v	Eq.(23) Adj.R^2	Eq.(23) S.E.	Eq.(24) Adj.R^2	Eq.(24) S.E.
2001/1/21 ~ 2003/6/30	1.869*** (0.407)	-0.067 (0.621)	---	0.944*** (0.014)	-0.005* (0.002)	---	0.938	8.014	0.903	0.456
	1.639*** (0.399)	-0.247 (0.627)	-0.00004 (0.0011)	0.942*** (0.013)	-0.009*** (0.003)	0.0009*** (0.0003)	0.941	7.814	0.908	0.443

(Note1) Numbers in parentheses are standard errors. ***/**/* denotes significance at the 1/5/10 percent level.

(Note2) ☐ indicates that the effect of quantitative easing is statistically significant and effective.

(Table 7)

Credit Spreads (1)

$$CS_t^i = \phi_i(IR_t) + \alpha_i(HV_{t-1}^i) + \delta_i(IV_t^s) + \beta_i(CA_t) + \gamma_i(OP_t) + c_i + \xi_t^i, \qquad (25)$$
$$\text{where } \delta_i = \gamma_i = 0.$$

	i	\multicolumn{4}{c}{Sample period: 2001/1/21 ~ 2003/6/30}	\multicolumn{4}{c}{Sample period: 2001/1/21 ~ 2004/3/31}
		ϕ_i	α_i	β_i	$adj.R^2/S.E.$	ϕ_i	α_i	β_i	$adj.R^2/S.E.$
Aa	1 year	0.0651*** (0.0010)	-0.7783*** (0.0431)	-0.0014*** (3.68E-05)	0.560 0.027	0.0540*** (0.0023)	-0.883*** (0.0857)	-0.0020*** (5.08E-05)	0.614 0.026
	3 year	0.0933*** (0.0011)	1.2627*** (0.0317)	-0.0031*** (5.35E-05)	0.750 0.031	0.1001*** (0.0037)	1.4986*** (0.0696)	-0.0026*** (6.67E-05)	0.773 0.029
	5 year	0.0931*** (0.0014)	0.9568*** (0.0348)	-0.0019*** (6.40E-05)	0.787 0.023	0.0963*** (0.0022)	0.8822*** (0.0587)	-0.0017*** (8.36E-05)	0.800 0.022
A	1 year	0.1835*** (0.0021)	-1.0513*** (0.0391)	0.0057*** (0.0001)	0.375 0.049	0.0328*** (0.0045)	-1.4361*** (0.0961)	-0.0034*** (0.0001)	0.297 0.061
	3 year	0.1237*** (0.0017)	-0.7448*** (0.0283)	0.0021*** (9.14E-05)	0.370 0.041	0.0362*** (0.0045)	-0.2600*** (0.0479)	-0.0033*** (0.0001)	0.412 0.048
	5 year	0.1275*** (0.0023)	3.2136*** (0.0587)	0.0010*** (0.0001)	0.349 0.056	0.0357*** (0.0062)	1.7938*** (0.109)	-0.0049*** (0.0001)	0.487 0.058
Baa	1 year	0.3084*** (0.0034)	1.6760*** (0.0581)	0.0131*** (0.0002)	0.372 0.084	0.0129 (0.0095)	4.2588*** (0.1944)	-0.0042*** (0.0002)	0.160 0.111
	3 year	0.2946*** (0.0033)	2.4108*** (0.0591)	0.0202*** (0.0002)	0.419 0.109	-0.0233 (0.0142)	3.7964*** (0.1821)	0.0006* (0.0003)	0.028 0.134
	5 year	0.3140*** (0.0034)	4.1787*** (0.0712)	0.0208*** (0.0002)	0.394 0.124	-0.0102 (0.0142)	6.1055*** (0.2393)	0.0010** (0.0004)	0.062 0.145
J-statistic		\multicolumn{4}{c}{0.0026}	\multicolumn{4}{c}{0.0053}

(Note1) Numbers in parentheses are standard errors. ***/**/* denotes significance at the 1/5/10 percent level.

(Note2) Instrumental variables of GMM;
constant term, $CS_{t-j}^i, HV_{t-j}^i, IR_{t-j}, CA_{t-j}$ $(j = 1,2,3)$

(Note3) Based on Hansen test, we do not statistically reject the overidentifying restrictions (at the 20% significance level) for each estimation.

(Note4) ☐ indicates the effect of quantitative easing is statistically significant and effective.
▨ indicates the effect of quantitative easing is statistically significant but harmful.

(Note5) We use a historical volatility of the credit spread CS_t^i over the past five business days ($k=5$).

$$HV_t^i = \sqrt{\frac{1}{k}\sum_{j=0}^{k-1}\left[CS_{t-j}^i - \frac{1}{k}\sum_{j=0}^{k-1}CS_{t-j}^i\right]^2}.$$

(Table 8)

Credit Spreads (2)

$$CS_t^i = \phi_i(IR_t) + \alpha_i(HV_{t-1}^i) + \delta_i(IV_t^s) + \beta_i(CA_t) + \gamma_i(OP_t) + c_i + \xi_t^i, \qquad (25)$$

$$\text{where } \delta_i = \beta_i = 0.$$

	i	ϕ_i	α_i	γ_i	$adj.R^2/S.E.$
		Sample period: 2001/1/21 ~ 2003/6/30			
Aa	1 year	-0.0034 (0.0027)	-1.3421*** (0.0862)	-0.0073*** (0.0002)	0.649 0.024
	3 year	0.0421*** (0.0047)	1.3461*** (0.0836)	-0.0081*** (0.0003)	0.765 0.031
	5 year	0.0426*** (0.0036)	0.8742*** (0.0661)	-0.0065*** (0.0003)	0.823 0.022
A	1 year	0.1730*** (0.0077)	-1.2902*** (0.0907)	0.0067*** (0.0004)	0.259 0.053
	3 year	0.1121*** (0.0069)	-0.8164*** (0.0580)	0.0019*** (0.0004)	0.342 0.042
	5 year	0.0697*** (0.0078)	2.9533*** (0.1241)	-0.0032*** (0.0004)	0.357 0.056
Baa	1 year	0.3524*** (0.0131)	2.3284*** (0.1375)	0.0211*** (0.0007)	0.229 0.094
	3 year	0.5157*** (0.0155)	2.0704*** (0.1515)	0.0440*** (0.0009)	0.386 0.112
	5 year	0.4480*** (0.0155)	4.776*** (0.1605)	0.0382*** (0.0009)	0.280 0.135
J-statistic		0.0056			

(Note1) Numbers in parentheses are standard errors. ***/**/* denotes significance at the 1/5/10 percent level.

(Note2) Instrumental variables of GMM;
constant term, CS_{t-j}^i, HV_{t-j}^i, IR_{t-j}, OP_{t-j} $(j = 1,2,3)$

(Note3) Based on Hansen test, we do not statistically reject the overidentifying restrictions (at the 20% significance level) for each estimation.

(Note4) ☐ indicates the effect of quantitative easing is statistically significant and effective.
▨ indicates the effect of quantitative easing is statistically significant but harmful.

(Note5) We use a historical volatility of the credit spread CS_t^i over the past five business days ($k=5$).

$$HV_t^i = \sqrt{\frac{1}{k}\sum_{j=0}^{k-1}\left[CS_{t-j}^i - \frac{1}{k}\sum_{j=0}^{k-1}CS_{t-j}^i\right]^2}.$$

(Table 9)

Credit Spreads (3)

$$CS_t^i = \phi_i(IR_t) + \alpha_i(HV_{t-1}^i) + \delta_i(IV_t^s) + \beta_i(CA_t) + \gamma_i(OP_t) + c_i + \xi_t^i, \qquad (25)$$

$$\text{where } \alpha_i = \gamma_i = 0.$$

	i	Sample period: 2001/1/21 ~ 2003/6/30				Sample period: 2001/1/21 ~ 2004/3/31			
		ϕ_i	δ_i	β_i	adj.R²/S.E.	ϕ_i	δ_i	β_i	adj.R²/S.E.
Aa	1 year	0.0576*** (0.0010)	-0.0012*** (3.55E-05)	-0.0017*** (4.66E-05)	0.579 0.027	0.0480*** (0.0016)	-0.0012*** (4.98E-05)	-0.0022*** (3.29E-05)	0.632 0.025
	3 year	0.0796*** (0.0014)	-0.0027*** (5.30E-05)	-0.0040*** (6.84E-05)	0.798 0.028	0.0984*** (0.0018)	-0.0027*** (7.84E-05)	-0.0030*** (4.06E-05)	0.810 0.026
	5 year	0.0922*** (0.0015)	0.1273*** (0.0033)	-0.0020*** (7.33E-05)	0.789 0.023	0.0969*** (0.0013)	-0.0005*** (4.72E-05)	-0.0017*** (4.22E-05)	0.801 0.022
A	1 year	0.1926*** (0.0025)	0.0021*** (0.0001)	0.0064*** (0.0001)	0.402 0.048	0.0319*** (0.0035)	0.0013*** (0.0001)	-0.0032*** (9.70E-05)	0.301 0.061
	3 year	0.1281*** (0.0022)	0.0010*** (7.39E-05)	0.0025*** (0.0001)	0.377 0.041	0.0367*** (0.0028)	0.0007*** (0.0001)	-0.0032*** (9.59E-05)	0.414 0.048
	5 year	0.1469*** (0.0032)	0.0032*** (0.0001)	0.0017*** (0.0001)	0.389 0.054	0.0447*** (0.0039)	0.0026*** (0.0001)	-0.0045*** (8.69E-05)	0.508 0.057
Baa	1 year	0.3300*** (0.0045)	0.0024*** (0.0002)	0.0141*** (0.0002)	0.383 0.084	0.0258*** (0.0071)	0.0008*** (0.0003)	-0.0041*** (0.0002)	0.152 0.111
	3 year	0.3265*** (0.0048)	0.0029*** (0.0002)	0.0218*** (0.0002)	0.424 0.109	-0.0055 (0.0098)	0.0013*** (0.0003)	0.0014*** (0.0002)	0.011 0.136
	5 year	0.3717*** (0.0053)	0.0057*** (0.0002)	0.0238*** (0.0003)	0.401 0.123	0.0165* (0.0096)	0.0040*** (0.0004)	0.0022** (0.0003)	0.023 0.148
J-statistic		0.0028				0.0033			

(Note1) Numbers in parentheses are standard errors. ***/**/* denotes significance at the 1/5/10 percent level.

(Note2) Instrumental variables of GMM;
constant term, CS_{t-j}^i, HV_{t-j}^i, IR_{t-j}, CA_{t-j} ($j = 1,2,3$)

(Note3) Based on Hansen test, we do not statistically reject the overidentifying restrictions (at the 20% significance level) for each estimation.

(Note4) ☐ indicates the effect of quantitative easing is statistically significant and effective.
▨ indicates the effect of quantitative easing is statistically significant but harmful.

(Table10)

Historical Volatilities of Credit Spreads

$$HV_t^i = \beta_{hv}^i CA_{t-k+1} + \gamma_{hv}^i OP_{t-k+1} + c^i + \mu_t^i \tag{26}$$

$$HV_t^i = \sqrt{\frac{1}{k}\sum_{j=0}^{k-1}\left[CS_{t-j}^i - \frac{1}{k}\sum_{j=0}^{k-1}CS_{t-j}^i\right]^2}$$

		β_{hv}^i (imposing $\gamma_{hv}^i = 0$)				γ_{hv}^i (imposing $\beta_{hv}^i = 0$)	
		Sample period: 2001/1/21~2003/6/30		Sample period: 2001/1/21~2004/3/31		Sample period: 2001/1/21~2003/6/30	
i		k=5	k=10	k=5	k=10	k=5	k=10
Aa	1 year	-1.3E-04*** (7.7E-06)	-1.8E-04*** (9.8E-06)	-5.3E-05*** (7.0E-06)	-6.5E-05*** (7.9E-06)	-2.0E-04*** (1.0E-05)	-2.8E-04*** (1.2E-05)
	3 year	-1.4E-04*** (1.2E-05)	-2.0E-04*** (1.3E-05)	-1.1E-05 (1.1E-05)	-2.4E-05** (1.0E-05)	-2.1E-04*** (1.4E-05)	-3.1E-04*** (1.5E-05)
	5 year	-5.9E-05*** (9.6E-06)	-7.1E-05*** (1.1E-05)	1.2E-05 (9.4E-06)	1.6E-05** (7.7E-06)	-1.1E-05*** (1.5E-05)	-1.3E-04*** (1.8E-05)
A	1 year	-1.4E-04*** (1.1E-05)	-1.7E-04*** (1.0E-05)	-5.5E-05*** (8.2E-06)	-6.4E-05*** (9.1E-06)	-2.0E-04*** (1.6E-05)	-2.9E-04*** (1.5E-05)
	3 year	-9.8E-05*** (1.5E-05)	-9.2E-05*** (1.3E-05)	2.9E-05* (1.5E-05)	6.4E-05*** (1.8E-05)	-1.2E-04*** (2.7E-05)	-9.8E-05*** (2.3E-05)
	5 year	-9.1E-05*** (1.6E-05)	-9.1E-05*** (1.5E-05)	-3.6E-05*** (1.2E-05)	-5.1E-05*** (1.5E-05)	-1.2E-04*** (2.9E-05)	-1.2E-04*** (3.4E-05)
Baa	1 year	-8.7E-05*** (1.6E-05)	-7.0E-05*** (1.6E-05)	-6.0E-05** (9.8E-06)	-7.2E-05** (1.2E-06)	-1.6E-04*** (1.6E-05)	-1.5E-04*** (1.6E-05)
	3 year	5.3E-05** (2.4E-05)	1.4E-04** (2.2E-05)	8.5E-05*** (6.5E-05)	1.5E-05*** (1.8E-05)	6.1E-05 (2.4E-05)	2.3E-04** (4.2E-05)
	5 year	3.6E-05 (2.7E-05)	1.3E-04*** (2.7E-05)	2.1E-05 (1.6E-05)	4.5E-05** (2.2E-05)	2.5E-05 (5.2E-05)	2.3E-04*** (5.2E-05)
J-statistic		0.031	0.014	0.028	0.013	0.031	0.014

(Note1) Numbers in parentheses are standard errors. ***/**/* denotes significance at the 1/5/10 percent level.

(Note2) ▢ indicates the effect of quantitative easing is statistically significant and effective.

(Note3) Instrumental variables of GMM;
 constant term, HV_{t-k-j}^i, IR_{t-k-j}, CA_{t-k-j} or OP_{t-k-j} $(j=0,1,2)$

(Note4) Based on Hansen test, we do not statistically reject the overidentifying restrictions (at the 20% significance level) for each estimation.

(Table11)

Cross-Sectional Differences in the Measures of Asset Returns

		Maturity	
		Short (1M)	Long (1Y, 3Y, 5Y)
Measured return	Ex-ante return		High-grade Corporate Bonds(-) Low-grade Corporate Bonds(+)
	Proxied by Ex-post return	Stock Return (+) Forward Exchange Premium (-)	

Note. The sign "+ (-)" indicates that the quantitative easing leads to the increase (decrease) in the risk premium.

(Figure 1)

Current Account Balance and Monetary Base

(1) Current Account Balance at the Bank of Japan

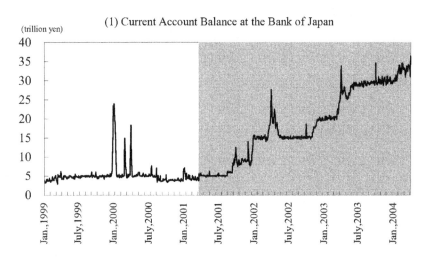

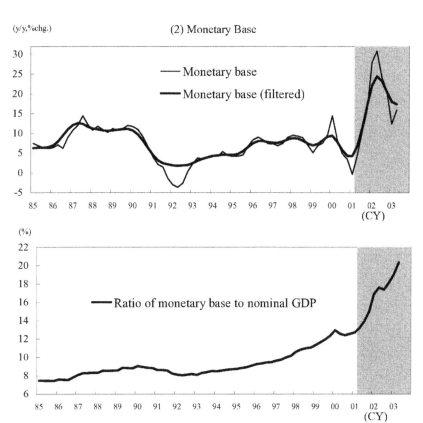

(Note) Shaded area indicates period under the quantitative easing.

(Figure 2)

Interest Rates

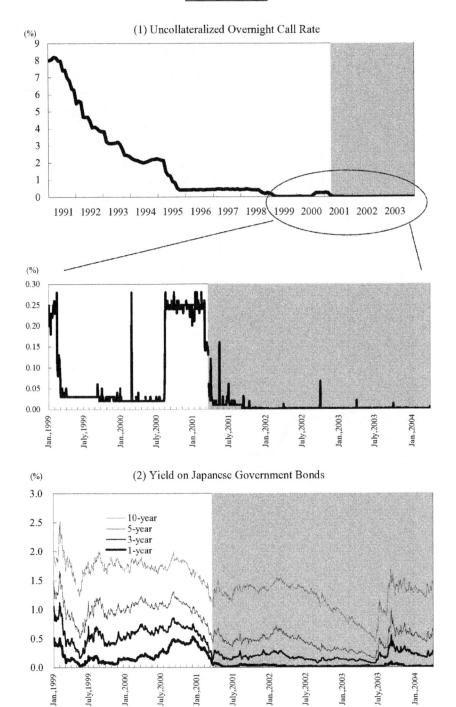

(1) Uncollateralized Overnight Call Rate

(2) Yield on Japanese Government Bonds

(Note) Shaded area indicates period under the quantitative easing.

(Figure 3)

Financial Asset Prices

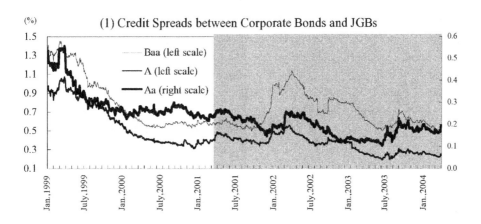

(1) Credit Spreads between Corporate Bonds and JGBs

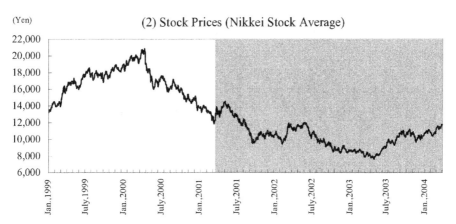

(2) Stock Prices (Nikkei Stock Average)

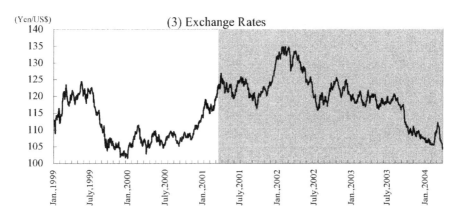

(3) Exchange Rates

(Note1) Credit spreads with 5-year maturity. Moody's ratings.
(Note2) Shaded area indicates period under the quantitative easing.

(Figure 4)

Risk Premiums and Credit Spreads

(%, annualized rate)   (1) Ex Post Risk Premium for Stock Return

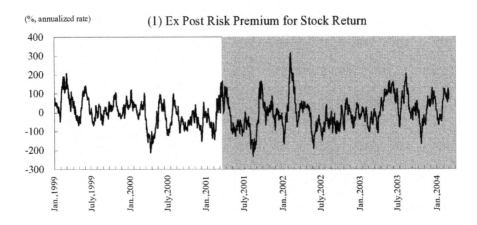

(%, annualized rate)   (2) Ex Post Forward Exchange Risk Premium

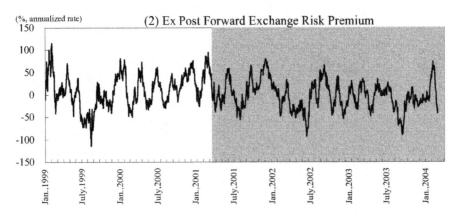

(%)   (3) Credit Spreads between Corporate Bonds and JGBs

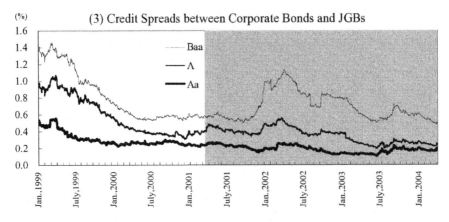

(Note1) Credit spreads with 5-year maturity. Moody's ratings.
(Note2) Shaded area indicates period under the quantitative easing.

(Figure 5)

Volatilities of Financial Asset Prices

(1 month, annualized rate, %)   (1) Implied Volatility of Stock Price

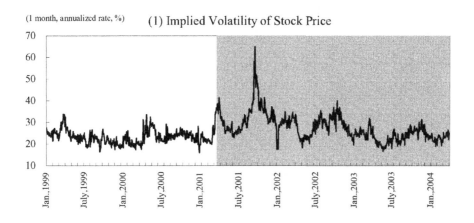

(1 month, annualized rate, %)   (2) Implied Volatility of Exchange Rate

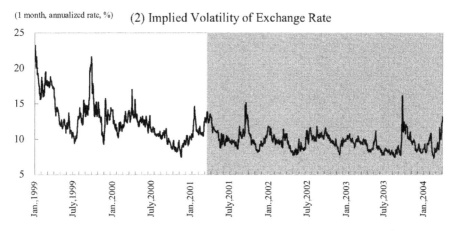

(%)   (3) Historical Volatilities of Credit Spreads

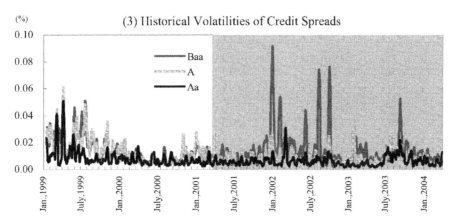

(Note1) Credit spreads with 5-year maturity. Moody's ratings.
(Note2) Shaded area indicates period under the quantitative easing.

(Figure 6)

BOJ's Balance Sheet and Outstanding of JGBs

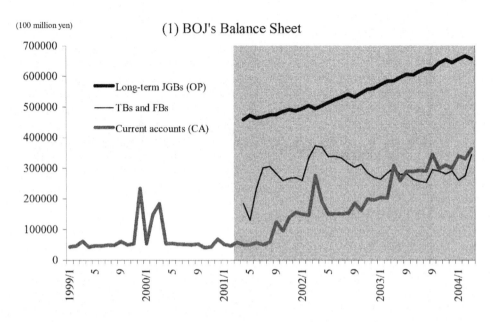

(1) BOJ's Balance Sheet

(100 million yen)

Long-term JGBs (OP)
TBs and FBs
Current accounts (CA)

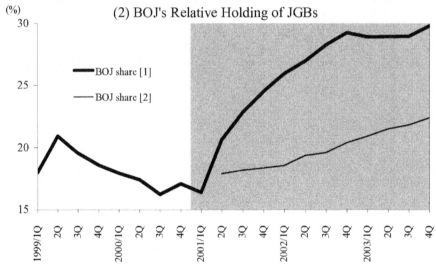

(%)

(2) BOJ's Relative Holding of JGBs

BOJ share [1]
BOJ share [2]

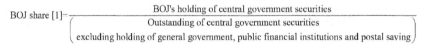

$$\text{BOJ share [1]} = \frac{\text{BOJ's holding of central government securities}}{\left(\begin{array}{c} \text{Outstanding of central government securities} \\ \text{excluding holding of general government, public financial institutions and postal saving} \end{array}\right)}$$

$$\text{BOJ share [2]} = \frac{\text{BOJ's holding of central government long-term securities}}{\left(\begin{array}{c} \text{Outstanding of central government long-term securities} \\ \text{including holding of general government, public financial institutions and postal saving} \end{array}\right)}$$

Data source: Bank of Japan, "Flow of Funds", "Bank of Japan Accounts". Ministry of Finance, "Japanese Government Bonds –Quarterly Newsletter–".

(Figure 7)

Business Cycle and Cross-Sectional Differences in Financial Asset Prices

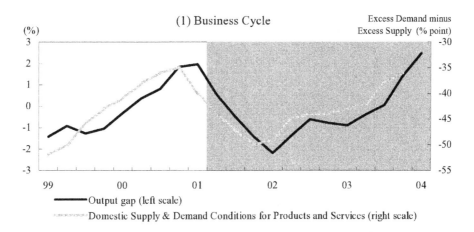

(1) Business Cycle

(%)

Excess Demand minus
Excess Supply (% point)

Output gap (left scale)

Domestic Supply & Demand Conditions for Products and Services (right scale)

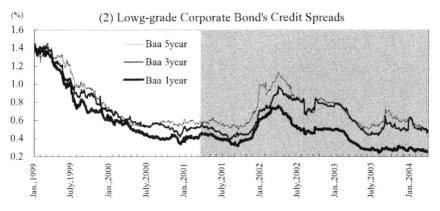

(2) Lowg-grade Corporate Bond's Credit Spreads

- Baa 5year
- Baa 3year
- Baa 1year

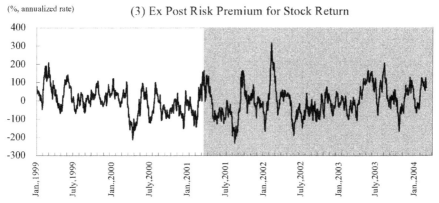

(%, annualized rate)

(3) Ex Post Risk Premium for Stock Return

(Note1) Output gap is estimated by using Hodrick-Prescott Filter. Domestic supply and demand conditions are based on Tankan Diffusion index ("Excess demand" minus "Excess supply").

(Note2) Credit spreads are based on Moody's ratings.

(Note3) Shaded area indicates period under the quantitative easing.

CPSIA information can be obtained at www.ICGtesting.com
Printed in the USA
BVOW07s0254081015

421436BV00007B/16/P